NOT MY
FIRST
RODEO

NOT MY FIRST RODEO

LESSONS FROM THE HEARTLAND

Kristi Noem

TWELVE

NEW YORK BOSTON

Twelve
Hachette Book Group
1290 Avenue of the Americas, New York, NY 10104
twelvebooks.com
twitter.com/twelvebooks

First Edition: June 2022

Twelve is an imprint of Grand Central Publishing. The Twelve name and logo are trademarks of Hachette Book Group, Inc.

The publisher is not responsible for websites (or their content) that are not owned by the publisher.

The Hachette Speakers Bureau provides a wide range of authors for speaking events. To find out more, go to www.hachettespeakersbureau.com or call (866) 376-6591.

Scripture quotations marked NIV are from the Holy Bible, New International Version®, NIV® Copyright ©1973, 1978, 1984, 2011 by Biblica, Inc.® Used by permission. All rights reserved worldwide. Scripture quotations marked NLT are from the *Holy Bible*, New Living Translation, copyright © 1996, 2004, 2015 by Tyndale House Foundation. Used by permission of Tyndale House Publishers, Inc., Carol Stream, Illinois 60188. All rights reserved. Scripture quotations marked NLV are taken from the *New Life Version*, copyright © 1969 and 2003. Used by permission of Barbour Publishing, Inc., Uhrichsville, Ohio 44683. All rights reserved. Scripture quotations marked ESV are from the *ESV® Bible (The Holy Bible, English Standard Version®)*, Copyright © 2001 by Crossway, a publishing ministry of Good News Publishers. Used by permission. All rights reserved. Scripture quotations marked NKJV are taken from the New King James Version®. Copyright © 1982 by Thomas Nelson. Used by permission. All rights reserved.

Library of Congress Control Number: 2022931304

ISBNs: 9781538707050 (hardcover), 9781538707074 (ebook)

Printed in the United States of America

LSC-C

Printing 1, 2022

For my mom, Corinne Arnold—the first to believe in me. She spoke life into me and helped me understand how special I am to God. Her encouragement let me know I could do anything; her love told me I was already enough.

Contents

Prologue   1

Chapter 1:   The Tapes   5

Chapter 2:   The Rugged Life   17

Chapter 3:   Riding with "TR"   27

Chapter 4:   Respect   33

Chapter 5:   No Herd Mentality   41

Chapter 6:   Burning Daylight   51

Chapter 7:   Love Is Patient   67

Chapter 8:   The Day We Lost Him   79

Chapter 9:   The Good Mess   97

Chapter 10: Rookie   109

Chapter 11: Nudges   123

Chapter 12: Outlaw at the Rodeo   135

Contents

Chapter 13:   Friend of the Farmer   149

Chapter 14:   Battling Bureaucrats—
                and Beetles   163

Chapter 15:   Beating the Beltway
                Mentality   175

Chapter 16:   Heading Home   189

Chapter 17:   A Hard Year   201

Chapter 18:   Tribal Trials   213

Chapter 19:   Girl Talk   225

Chapter 20:   Principles for a Pandemic   231

Chapter 21:   America's Fireworks   249

Epilogue   265

Acknowledgments   267

About the Author   271

NOT MY
FIRST
RODEO

Prologue

W e don't complain about things, Kristi. We fix them."

These words, so often spoken by my dad, have motivated me to show up for the tough jobs in my life. From cleaning stalls to signing legislation.

Growing up on a farm in South Dakota, there was always plenty that needed fixing. The same is true of our world. God gives us all different talents to work on our own little corner of it. We ought to do so humbly—our society is so hungry for that—but we shouldn't shy away from debate, and we shouldn't settle for an easy out that leaves the job for someone else later.

That's partly why I got into politics in the first place, not exactly a profession I ever envisioned as a young girl pulling calves on the ranch or competing in rodeos across the state. While politics has been anything but easy, convenient, or pleasant, it was, I believe, the right choice. But I will let you be the judge on that one.

I am the first woman to serve as governor of South

Dakota. While this is deeply significant to me, I do not believe there are "women's issues" any more than there are "men's issues." There are only issues that affect us all as Americans. There is, however, a woman's perspective on *every single issue*. That perspective is essential when we as a country make decisions about our freedom, defense, prosperity, health, and the well-being and happiness of our kids.

I've offered that perspective—whether people asked for it or not—from the barnyard to Congress. Always with conviction. Often, alone.

Along the way I've learned a few things. I often tell young people one of the best things they can do is decide to be a teachable person. You can learn something from everyone, even your worst critic. This book is my attempt to share some of what I've learned about family, work, faith, and decision-making.

Fair warning: this is a memoir of a life so far; it is *not* a book about politics. Of course, campaigns and political fights—from South Dakota's windswept plains to the marbled halls of Congress—make up a good part of these pages. But politics is a lot like walking through a feedlot in springtime: it's slow going and you're constantly surrounded by crap. Who wants to read that?

You'll find some familiar faces here—presidents and politicians. You'll find relatively unknown people who are every ounce as important. But the character on every page is South Dakota. It is my home. It has made me who I am. After a global pandemic and the crisis in American cities, more and more people are discovering the gift of rural life, learning that it's better for their families—and for their souls. Rural communities are at the heart of our American story: they are people taking risks to earn a living off the land. If these memories and stories do nothing more than make you want to come see South Dakota, to be among its honest, hardworking people for a moment or a lifetime, that's good enough for me.

But if you happen to learn a little more about the daughter of a farmer who can't help choosing the hard way at every turn...

About a rodeo queen who prefers cowboy boots to high heels...

About a wife, mother, and grandmother who has, by now, learned a thing or two about politics in America...

Well, at least you'll be entertained. Life is a rodeo. Hang on.

Kristi
Christmas 2021

Chapter 1

The Tapes

I don't know why I'm doing this," he said over the crackles of the tape recorder. "I guess I'll go check cows."

Click.

The tape stopped. That was the end.

I couldn't believe what I had just heard, what I had just found, what I held in my hands. And what a gift it was.

Suddenly, I knew everything was going to be okay. We were going to get through this.

Just a few months before I discovered the tapes, my dad, Ron Arnold, died in an accident on our farm. I was twenty-two, newly married, pregnant with our first child, and taking classes at South Dakota State University forty-five minutes away. One day, I finally got the courage to go clean out his pickup.

Now, everyone who has a farmer or a rancher in their family knows they live out of their pickups. Everything important can be found in the cab, including wallets, bills to pay, cattle and seed records. The console is littered with dusty little notes about things that need to be done, jotted down on whatever may be handy—food wrappers, scrap paper, or cardboard from a tool package.

The little microcassettes mixed in the jumble of odds and ends in Dad's console, however, contained something more important than just his latest, fleeting to-do list. They were something he clearly wanted to leave behind. They were kind of a record of everything he had done and how he did it.

Dad's truck was his office. It was his desk. His filing cabinet. His library. As every farmer's kid knows, if you need to find something important, the first place you look is in the cab of his pickup.

But since the accident, I just could not bring myself to go clean out his truck. It was just too hard. Now, I am not a sappy person. I don't get particularly emotional about things. I am not a procrastinator. If something needs doing, I just go do it. But this was the hardest thing I ever had to do in my life.

I was still in shock that he was gone.

My dad was indestructible. He never quit and never let anything stop him. I remember sitting at his funeral days after the accident and staring at his casket. He was forty-nine when he died. I thought to myself, *Yep, he's going to sit up any minute. No way he is really dead. He is going to sit up and tell us to get back to work.*

Those were hard days. I was devastated. I had lost my anchor.

But there were also more pressing problems for my family and me. How were we going to keep it all going? How were we going to make a living? Would we be able to keep the farm afloat? Every day was filled with thousands of questions to which I had no answers.

What seed should we plant? What field to plant first? What is the price we need for our calves to keep the cattle operation running? What neighbor is giving me the best advice?

It was overwhelming, and I was not handling it well. I could not sleep. I got real quiet and kept my thoughts to myself. I did the only thing I really knew how to do, which was work. And I worked hard.

Obviously, I was not the only one suffering. And I wasn't any help in that department. According to my family, I got hard and angry and, at times, downright mean. My mom kept telling me I needed to grieve. Well, I didn't want to. I didn't even know what that meant. I just wanted to work. I wanted to be outside, doing what Dad always did. Work was the only thing that provided me with a bit of peace, a moment of respite from the overwhelming dread I had about the future. I literally had no idea how we were going to keep this family business going without my dad. Worst of all, I could see it in the neighbors' eyes when they came over to check on us or chatted with me at the sale barn or grain elevator. They also were worried we wouldn't make it.

The easiest thing to do probably would have been to sell everything and find a new line of work. Take a break and figure out a new future. But in my head I could hear Dad's voice saying to me: "Don't ever sell land, Kristi. God isn't making any more land."

Hearing Dad's voice in my head seemed natural, because the truth is I'm a whole lot like him. I am not afraid of hard work. I am strong and even more strong-willed. As my husband, Bryon, likes to say, "You always pick the hardest option. There will be three options and you always pick the most impossible one. That's really hard to be married to."

Turns out Bryon is pretty tough too. We have been married thirty years now.

Walking out of the house that day to clean out Dad's truck, I was determined we were not going to fail. I was not going to let everything Dad had built blow away. Somehow, some way, we were going to make it. Or I was going to die trying. I just had no idea where to begin. Honestly, in the months since he had died, I'd been faking my way through each and every day. And I was scared.

But as I carried an empty box out to his truck, I was focused on the job at hand. I opened the middle console between the two front-seat captain's chairs and found the tiny silver tape recorder, the kind that doctors dictate into. This was a surprise for sure. I had never seen it before and had no idea why he had it or what might be on the tapes.

I popped in a cassette and pushed Play. It was my dad's voice, talking—as if he were sitting right there in the front seat of his truck with me. That was a pretty haunting moment.

On that first tape, Dad was explaining seed corn varieties and which ones performed best on specific fields we owned and others we rented. He talked about how the extra-wet year before had resulted in poor crop yields and damaged grain. He said the harvest was tough, and he went on to describe the variety of choices he would have made differently and what he thought might work better for the spring we were expecting.

Sitting there in the driver's seat of my dad's truck, my eyes started to fill with tears as I listened to his voice from the past.

Digging deeper through all the junk in the console, I found more tiny, clear cassette tapes—about a dozen in all, each in its own little plastic case. One by one, through eyes blurred by tears, I slipped each into the recorder and listened to him talk about cows, weather, and crops, and what to do if we ever found ourselves in a tough financial situation.

I have always believed in the power of prayer. And I have always been okay with how prayers are often answered in ways we least suspect, rarely answered in any kind of direct way. Sometimes we really have to hunt for the answers to prayers.

But this was something else. Here I was in the hardest, most hopeless, most impossible moment of my entire life. Like storm clouds parting, never before had my prayers been answered so directly and clearly. And it was all in my dad's voice.

On each of those tapes were the answers to so many of the questions I had asked over and over in the months since he had died. How many times had I said to myself, "If only I could just ask Dad this one question." Here were all the answers, straight from him, in *his* voice—literally in the palm of my hand.

I started to sob. I completely lost it. I might have been "grieving," but in that moment I wasn't exactly sad. It was more like a revelation and a relief.

For the first time since he'd died, after months of going through all the motions and pretending things were fine, I realized with absolute certainty that we were going to make it. I and my mom and my sister and my brothers, we were going to be okay.

The words in my dad's voice came straight from God, telling me, "I will provide. Stop worrying. You will be okay. Your family will be okay. I've got this."

A peace like I had never felt before in my life passed over me. And to this day—no matter what this crazy world throws at me—I think back to that summer day, sitting in my dad's dusty truck, listening to his voice as an answer to my most desperate prayers. It gives me strength and I know we will be okay.

Listening to all the tapes, I got to the last one. It ended with Dad, as usual, getting restless. He was eager to get on with work. He paused for a moment.

"I don't know why I'm doing this," he said impatiently. "I guess I'll go check cows."

All these years later I still think of that and laugh to myself. He might not have known in that moment exactly why he was talking into a microcassette inside a tiny little tape recorder in the cab of his truck. But not a day goes by that I don't give thanks that he did.

Included in those tapes was one that was several years old.

Now, dad drove his trucks hard, racked up miles, and always traded them in before they started to break down or had close to one hundred thousand miles on them. We had a lot of old equipment and trucks around the ranch. But he needed one vehicle that would never leave him stranded anywhere. It had to be reliable. So, buying a new pickup often wasn't some kind of luxury. It was an absolute necessity.

My point is, the tape that was several years old when I played it for the first time had seen the inside of several different truck consoles. It had been moved from pickup to pickup for years.

That tape was different from the others in that he wasn't talking about just the weather, cows, and grain prices. He talked about us kids. Me, my sister, Cindy, and my two brothers, Rock and Robb. At the time he recorded that tape, most of us were teenagers. He spoke of our strengths, our weaknesses, what he thought we struggled with, and what he thought we would be when we grew up.

You could hear in his voice that he wondered what he could do to help us be better people and succeed in life. (Now, my dad was not exactly Dr. Phil. He didn't sit around watching Oprah Winfrey all day. And, like me, he wasn't emotional about anything. But nobody ever loved his kids more than Dad loved us in his tough way.) What surprised me most in that tape was his insight into what made each of his kids tick. What our passions were and what habits or behaviors in each of us he feared would cripple us for life if we didn't deal with them at an early age.

He talked about how tough he thought I was, and whether I knew it. I can tell you that growing up I tried so hard to please him and—as a kid—I never felt like I did enough. I always felt I could and *should* do better, be better, work harder.

As much as I was like my dad, I could tell from that tape that he knew my strengths *and* my flaws. But he sure loved each one of us for exactly who we were. I had no idea my dad ever spent time thinking about us this way or dreamed about us and our futures. Here I was at twenty-two years of age, listening to my deceased father describe me as a fourteen-year-old and what he thought I could be when I grew up. I wish I had known his thoughts earlier. I wish we would have talked more. I wish we would have argued less about the stupid things that two hardheaded, willful people find to fight about. More than anything, I just wish I'd had more time with him. I wish the world could have seen all he would have done if he had not died so young. And I wish he would have lived to see all of his kids grow into adults and make new lives of their own. I wish he could have seen his grandchildren, could have watched them grow up.

On that day, listening to my dad talk about a future he would not live to see, I made a decision about my own life. I vowed to never waste my time on things that do not ultimately matter. I would live every day with purpose. I aimed to serve my family, my neighbors, my state, and my country in any way I could. I would not follow the glittery distractions of whatever was popular or convenient at any given moment. I pledged to be honest and straightforward in all things, no matter how hard it might be or how harsh the truth might sound to those around me. No doubt my husband, Bryon, is right. It *does* make life hard. But as I learned that day, what matters is not how hard life is, but rather how hard you fight for what is right—and how tall you stand against what is wrong.

Like my dad, I aim to stand fast in any current for what I believe.

That is why I got into politics. It was not the easy, convenient, or pleasant choice. But it was, I believe, the right choice.

If you want to find heaven on earth, it's in northeastern South Dakota, where I grew up. You have never seen skies like those stretching over these endless rolling hills, deep blue and dotted with clouds—except when the storms come. *Then* you won't find a more fearsome display of nature's power anywhere in the world. Our part of the state receives much more rain than the western part. Our glittering rivers give proof of that.

This was where we had our farm. Growing up, I *loved* our farm. I thought it was amazing. Always immaculately kept, mowed, with white fences that went on and on. Nice, neat buildings. No weeds or junk lying about. As kids, we spent most of our childhood pulling weeds, painting fences, and mowing grass. We were taught to take pride in our work.

There was a magazine my parents subscribed to when I was a child that had a monthly series called "Prettiest Place in the Country." I waited for that magazine every month because I loved reading those articles and looking at the pictures of the beautiful farms and ranches across America. I *dreamed* of our farm being in that magazine. I even wrote a couple of letters to the editors asking them to come and visit our farm because I was sure that if they just saw it for themselves, they would recognize that it clearly belonged in their pages to showcase to the world what a truly beautiful farm looked like. They never wrote back.

At the other end of our state lies one of the proudest features of South Dakota—Mount Rushmore. It is a stunning monument to four great men who founded this country, saved us from total destruction, and did so much to preserve America with all her limitless potential: George Washington, Thomas Jefferson, Abraham Lincoln, and Teddy Roosevelt. Four of the finest men to ever live.

Goodness knows they were not perfect.

America is great because the people who came before us and built this country were imperfect. And they knew it. Their obvious imperfections gave them humility. That is why they envisioned a country where no single imperfect person—or small group of imperfect people—would have all the power. Instead, all of us—imperfect as we all are—would come together and work on problems together and figure things out together. While each and every one of us is imperfect, the final result of that democratic, constitutional process would achieve the most perfect solutions possible.

America did not just happen. It wasn't an accident. We are here not because of one king, one group of powerful oligarchs, one race, or one set of ancestral boundaries. America is the most powerful, prosperous country in the world because we, the people, have worked together through a democratic, constitutional process.

These gifts of freedom, self-determination, and individual liberty were not easily won. That took guts, blood, and vision. Brave people, guided by great purpose, fought for these gifts. For them, the future was never certain. Nothing was guaranteed. Yet they gambled everything, risked their lives, and put their fortunes on the line for the principles they believed in. The result of their daring efforts was the single greatest experiment in freedom and self-governance in human history.

Just like the tapes my dad left me, we have been blessed with a great inheritance.

And whether my family's farm or our country, I'm going to fight to preserve it.

Chapter 2

The Rugged Life

I was born in Watertown, South Dakota. My parents, Ron and Corinne Arnold, had a bit of a scare when I was born because the umbilical cord was wrapped around my neck and I wasn't breathing. Obviously, they got it all worked out because here I am. When I was younger Mom used to call me her "little miracle." Much later, my family joked that the only reason I got into politics was because that cord around my neck had cut off the flow of oxygen to my brain.

Nobody in our house was allowed to take themselves too seriously. But there was also a lot of love. We lived in a modest but comfortable house. Our social life revolved around mostly church at the Family Worship Center in Watertown, and the community and schools in Hamlin County, named for President Lincoln's vice president.

My parents both grew up in South Dakota. On their first

date, Dad took Mom to a Lowell Lundstrom revival on a Wednesday night. They got married and settled on the same land where Dad's parents lived and where Dad had learned to farm. We raised cattle and grew corn, soybeans, wheat, and alfalfa. Dad rotated barley or flax when the market seemed good. We had horses, of course, and also raised buffalo for a time, as well as a random assortment of 4-H sheep and the occasional goat. Farming, hunting, and riding horses was pretty much in our blood, like it is for a lot of families—especially out here in the Midwest.

While I grew up on a ranch, my childhood was probably not all that different from the way kids all over America grow up in terms of school, church, sports, hunting, rodeo, and family. But from the time I was a little girl I felt kind of out of place, like I didn't belong. I was uncomfortable with who I was and always very aware of my shortcomings. I guess, like a lot of children, I lacked confidence when I was young. Most people are surprised to find out I am an introvert. I mean, look at my day-to-day life now. I spend all my time talking with people, giving speeches, attending events, doing media interviews—all activities that involve being very outward focused, always being ready, being "on," performing and giving a good impression—hopefully. But that does not come naturally for me. In fact, I find it pretty exhausting. Don't get me wrong, I love people and I love what I do. But if I need a day that "fixes" me, if I need to recharge, my natural inclination is to go sit in a tree stand and hunt deer or spend time outside in some activity that involves animals and nature. Being alone is something I can find joy in.

Being quiet is a gift.

As the third of four children in a busy house on a working farm in northeastern South Dakota, there were quiet days, but no boring days. We were always working, it seemed. Growing up, I always thought that my mom and dad had had four children because they needed more hired hands to work on the farm and ranch. That's a joke—kind of.

I was a tomboy and I loved growing up on a farm. I loved animals and quickly adopted any kind of animal I could lay my hands on—in addition to the livestock that was part of our farming operation. At some point, I became known as the kid that would take in any random pet or abandoned animal. Most often these were raccoons. One of my very favorite pets was Bandi, a raccoon I raised from just a few days old that was a part of our family for more than ten years. I also had parakeets. And I was not terribly creative at naming them. They were Nicky 1, Nicky 2, and Nicky 3.

One chore that I never minded was feeding the dog and cats. I maintained a small herd of cats—usually between twenty and thirty of them—out in the barn.

Dad's barn was also a good place for keeping animals we were raising for 4-H contests and caring for any animals that had gotten hurt or were abandoned, or didn't find a home somewhere else when they needed one. That is how I ended up with my first burro, a long-haired goat, a miniature horse, and a sheep.

I am still amazed that my parents put up with all of it.

My birthday gifts included parakeets and puppies, including a shih tzu that couldn't hunt or help herd cows, but that dearly loved me. I was even granted permission to have a house cat. To my dad's great irritation, she wound up getting pregnant from some rendezvous with an outdoor cat. That cat gave birth to eight kitties underneath my dad's desk in his office. As you can imagine, he was having none of that. As many times as I moved them out and made the perfect spot for her somewhere else, she would have them back and snuggled in under his desk within the hour. He eventually gave up and I still love thinking about those tiny little kittens playing with Dad's socks and his wiggling toes while he worked on paperwork late into the night.

Mom was equally long-suffering in all my animal adoptions. She certainly did not appreciate all the frogs and salamanders I brought home from my explorations. Perhaps most disturbing for her was when I brought home baby mice I found and then wanted her to help me save their lives. She always did. Her patience with me and my animals was amazing. My mom has an incredible ability to see the unique gifts in everyone and she recognized my affinity to work with animals early on. I am sure she wished I would comb my hair once in a while and quit wearing my brothers' clothes, but she let me cut my hair short so it would not be a bother and focused on helping me see what I was good at.

Mom also let me learn what I *wasn't* so good at, and one of those things was music. Mom herself was a huge country music fan; she loved listening to Willie Nelson, Johnny Cash, and Waylon Jennings. I probably know every single country music song from that generation because she sang them in the car the whole way anywhere we went. With Mom's encouragement, I played piano for six years, but my fingers just don't work that way. Eventually, I switched to trumpet because it had only three buttons, and I figured I could handle that.

When I was in middle school, my dad offered me a deal: "Kristi, if you get to be first chair in the school band, I'll buy you a brand-new silver trumpet." I'd had my eye on that trumpet for a while, and I guess Dad was hoping that I'd either get better at practicing or else move on altogether. I did neither, but I did make first chair in the school band, and Dad was true to his word. That silver trumpet was a lot better than the rental I used to take out to the pasture and play for my horses. I'd sit on a fence rail and play and play, and the horses would stand right by me and listen. If you know horses at all, you know they are sensitive to loud noises. It is a miracle they could stand all my racket. Nobody else on our farm ever could.

I was a big reader growing up. Laura Ingalls Wilder was a favorite, of course, and when I got older, I devoured Louis L'Amour westerns. I especially loved the strong, silent characters who always followed their convictions, did what was right, and generally spoke little.

I think one of the reasons I liked them so much was that I was born without a filter, according to my mother. I remember my mouth getting washed out with soap many times during my childhood for saying something I should not have or talking back to those in authority. I distinctly remember being shocked by it each and every time.

What did I say? Are you kidding me? How am I possibly in trouble for my tone?

When I first went into politics, my family was the most surprised and admitted later that they spent a lot of time worrying about my mouth and the things I might say that could get me into trouble.

My sister, Cindy, is the oldest, and to my childhood eyes she was perfect. She was beautiful, sweet, kind, and never seemed to make a mistake. She worked outside, but she also helped my dad with bookkeeping and organizing his office. She worked with Mom, sorting the logistics of getting farm parts, food, or supplies out to the field for the entire operation. We had a very large farming operation, and it was constantly changing. It was nothing to bump into a new hire in the shop that Dad had just brought on that day. It was not unusual to be sent out to the yard to move a tractor or a truck Dad had just acquired. If it had a key and a gas pedal, you just had to figure it out. More than once one of us was sent out to some field having no idea how to get there because Dad had just rented it that day.

Keep up and figure it out. And don't come back until the job is done.

Cindy often got the "less dirty" jobs, but that was due more to her skill set and the fact that right behind Cindy were three other siblings who were able to fill in everywhere else. Cindy could sing like an angel, always obeyed our parents' rules, and didn't seem to get into trouble. She excelled at everything she did. We had to share a room growing up, and some of our biggest disagreements as sisters came because she was neat as a pin and I was, in her words, a "slob." Also, I loved wearing her clothes to school without asking. And, supposedly, I got them all dirty and never put them back.

My older brother, Rock, was the mechanic. Like my dad, he could fix anything and build almost anything. My childhood is filled with memories of him rewiring dirt bikes, snowmobiles, and engines to get more power out of them. He admired Evel Knievel, so many of our free afternoons were spent trying to figure out how to build better ramps and get the speed necessary to reach new heights. Rock was often scraped up or bruised, but that never seemed to stop him from taking chances after spending hours puzzling out his daredevil stunts.

Rock had severe asthma as a child and was sometimes rushed to the hospital for emergency treatments and in some cases would need to spend a night or two recovering. Living on a farm during harvest was extremely dangerous for him, as the dust could close up his airways in minutes. My mom had to closely monitor Rock.

My younger brother, Robb, was the baby. Robb was fun, but then what youngest child isn't? Like most parents, Mom and Dad were more lenient with the baby. They had quit overreacting to the small stuff that would have gotten us older kids in trouble. Perhaps that allowed Robb to become more independent and happy-go-lucky. He was naturally good at everything. If you gave him something to do, he would be an expert in five minutes. When he was eleven years old, he drove a tractor the two miles to elementary school sometimes because he was too young to legally drive a car. And if the tractor wouldn't start, he hopped on a four-wheeler instead and drove that to school. He could shoot better than anyone, drive better than everyone, and just had overall amazing luck and natural talent.

One of the best examples of Robb's luck came years later, when I asked my brothers for help filling my deer tag. I love to hunt. My brothers are always willing to take me along on their hunting trips out of the state, but most of the time we hunted on our own land during deer season in South Dakota.

Life was busy that particular fall with work and being married and raising kids. I hadn't had much time to hunt big game, so when I finally got my new license, I knew I might need a little help from my brothers. They kept up with all the big bucks around our farm, and they knew their habits and patterns in the area.

First, I got Rock to take me hunting. We spent a few days together. We would get up hours before daylight, sit in snowbanks or tree belts, high in tree stands on windy days, with gusts blowing over 20 mph and temps below zero. We stalked, scoped, and tried to outthink the deer. For all our efforts, we came up with nothing. Never even fired off a single shot.

I decided to change tactics. Sometimes with hunting or fishing you just need to try something different. A different size of shot in your shotgun and change up your gear. So I asked Robb to take me with him.

It was the night before the last day of the season, and Robb was not excited about it. Getting up that early to fill his own tag was obviously something he was willing to do. In fact, he had already done that, days earlier. But doing that for his sister was just a pain. He did not understand why I couldn't just go by myself and get the job done.

Yet he agreed and we set a time for me to pick him up the next morning. When I got to his house before daylight, he was still sitting at his kitchen table getting dressed. Slowly pulling on his socks and tugging his sweatshirt over his head. I was trying not to look nervous, but I could see the sun starting to come up and worried I was missing my opportunity to take advantage of the last day to fill my tag. Finally, he was ready and he climbed inside his pickup and quietly shut the door. I jumped in and slammed my door. His head snapped toward me and he whispered, "Quiet!"

Relax, I thought. We were literally sitting in the middle of the farmyard right in front of his house! Who did he think was going to hear us? He put his truck into drive and we started to slowly roll across the yard and down the driveway headed east without our lights on. The sun was starting to come up.

We drove no more than three minutes, about a mile before he stopped. Robb looked out into the field and said, "Why don't you shoot that one?"

Peering through the half-light, I could make out a good-sized buck in the middle of the field. I nodded to Robb.

"Let's wait a couple of minutes for it to get lighter and then you can get out and shoot him," he said nonchalantly.

We sat there quietly in his truck, waiting for the sun to come up a little more.

After a few minutes, he said, "Okay. Get out and *don't slam the door*!"

He looked at me like I was a dummy. I got out slowly, kneeled in a ditch, and shot the buck. We had literally been hunting for fifteen minutes. We had spent fourteen of those minutes in the warm comfort of the truck cab. I had taken less than ten steps. But I had my deer. We had gotten the job done.

Robb's luck paid off for me.

Chapter 3

Riding with "TR"

To this day Theodore Roosevelt is a revered figure in the American West, and especially the Dakotas, where he spent several formative years before assuming the presidency at the relatively young age of forty-two. Roosevelt understood that time on your own in rugged country has a way of strengthening the body, mind, and spirit. "Rugged individualism" is a term we throw around a lot these days, but to "TR" it was something he learned by giving up a coddled life as a member of the New York City elite and going out west. Bravery and daring of the kind he showed in riding up San Juan Hill is highly prized on the plains by cowboys today. It is regarded as a timeless badge of character.

That explains why, in South Dakota, one of our favorite weekend pastimes is a good old-fashioned rodeo. Sure, there are clowns and corny jokes. But it's more than that.

It is a celebration of the American spirit—the bravery it takes to wrangle tough animals is the same raw human spirit that forged the nation. If TR were to visit a rodeo today, he would completely understand it. He would fit right in—and he'd probably want to hop on a bronc himself.

I think my dad and TR would have been pretty good friends if they'd had the opportunity to meet. They both loved the rugged life and pushed themselves to the limit, despite health challenges. They both loved America. And one thing was for sure: they both liked to be the boss.

Ron Arnold was a true cowboy. He was tough—the toughest person I have ever known. Ever since I was a little girl, I wanted to be just like him. He worked hard, said little, and demanded excellence from himself and everyone else. He was satisfied with only 100 percent of your effort. The guy was pure grit.

Dad was smart, and he could figure anything out. He could build most things and rebuild anything else. If he didn't build it, he could make it better. But most of all, he was tough. His hands were gnarled from a lifetime of work. So was his back—mostly from breaking horses.

You might think all that hard, dusty work might scare a kid away. Just the opposite. He was where all the excitement was. With Dad, you got to herd cattle, sell grain, and buy seed.

There were always treats that went along with all that hard work. If you were with Dad, you might pick rock all day in the field in 90-degree heat, but you were probably also going to get to drive the tractor; and at some point in the day, you were guaranteed to get ice cream. Banana splits or blackberry malts, paired with a hot can of 7UP pulled from the backseat of his pickup or a days-old plastic-packaged cinnamon roll with melted icing that may or may not be moldy. Nothing tasted better to a kid who had spent the day covered in dirt working in the field or chasing cows.

In the mornings, Dad would sometimes wake us kids up by teasingly yelling up the stairs, "Get up! More people die in bed than anywhere else!"

And once you were out of bed it was go, go, go.

Dad walked fast, and he insisted you walk beside him, so we ran everywhere we went. Even if he just sent you across the yard to pick something up for him, you did not walk. You sprinted. And he challenged you to anticipate what he needed before he asked for it. He wasn't just teaching us how to "do" something; he was teaching us to be thinkers as well. To be problem solvers.

And he never stopped trying to figure out how to make things work better, faster, and more efficiently. Dad rented farmland wherever he could find it because when you're a farmer more land is always better. He was always willing to rent land a couple of counties over. That meant he was always trying to figure out how to be more efficient because time was his most valuable commodity. How do you plant faster? How do you harvest quicker? How do you save time and money?

We had those huge green twelve-row corn planters you've probably seen if you've ever driven a highway in farm country. But John Deere didn't make those planters large enough for Dad at the time. He wanted a bigger one that he could pull with a tractor and cover more acres in less time. He bought two twelve-row corn planters and then built a hitch so he could pull both together at the same time behind the tractor, *twenty-four rows at a time*. It was a spectacle. And when people passing by saw it in a field, they often slowed down to watch it work.

One time he was driving down the road with my sister, Cindy, in the passenger seat, and he came up with a new plan for saving time.

"I'm going to invent a toothbrush," he told her.

According to him, people were forced into unnecessary steps every morning while brushing their teeth because all the equipment involved was not needed. You have the brush and you have the tube of toothpaste. Dad's idea was to make a toothbrush that stored all the toothpaste in the handle. That way, you could just squeeze the handle and the paste would squirt out into the bristles and you could brush your teeth, all one-handed.

"Think of all the time you would save!" he told Cindy.

Cindy hated to tell him it had already been invented.

While Dad was larger than life and tougher than nails, Mom was soft and kind. In so many ways, Mom kept us alive.

She grew up in Watertown, population approximately twenty thousand. She probably had no idea what she was getting into when she married my dad. Within weeks of becoming his bride, she found herself on a farm in the middle of nowhere, driving tractors, pulling calves, and miles away from everything she had ever known.

I think one of her most important roles was that of mediator between her children and her husband. Dad was so driven, he didn't have time to do all the things kids need. Mom explained to us why Dad was always in such a hurry and sometimes came off harsh. The weather was working against us. The markets were down. The cattle were fighting off disease. The bank was demanding payment. Taxes were going up. It never ended.

It didn't exactly help that Dad was constantly adding more acres and more head of cattle to try to spread out his costs and achieve a better return. To make it work, all he needed to do was find more hours in the day. More risk meant more rewards. It also meant more stress and pressure. He was always trying to think of ways to speed things up and grow his business. He often said his dream was for his farm and ranch to be big enough that all four of us kids could stay and be a part of the family business if we wanted to.

When Dad insisted that the combines never stop to empty the hopper during harvest, that meant we needed a new grain cart so they could dump on the go. At thirteen years old, I found myself driving a four-wheel-drive tractor and grain cart in a field with five combines going at full speed.

Operators were calling me on the radio to hurry up and get to them wherever they were in the field because they were getting full. I would pull up within inches of them without stopping and let them empty into my cart before heading full speed to the next combine that was waiting. I never stopped and when someone had to wait, I felt the pressure.

It wasn't long before almost all the farmers in our area were adding grain carts to their operations too.

Chapter 4

Respect

We were not terribly political growing up. We rarely spoke of leaders in Washington or whatever policies were being debated on the news. Political opinions were not something we discussed much. It wasn't like anybody wanted to grow up to be a politician or anything. We were into farming and growing things and raising animals and getting work done. We hunted. We believed every life had value and voted that way. We went to church every time the doors were open and obeyed the law—at least most of the time.

The politics on our ranch were lived out. We didn't talk about it; we just did it. Political parties, policy debates, politicians, and government didn't really fit into our daily lives in any obvious sort of way—except when suddenly they did. As I got older, I realized that whether we liked it or not, government and politics were part of life. The only question was:

What did I want to do with government and politics? And what did I think good government looked like?

If I had to describe my overall political beliefs—and the political beliefs of my whole family and most of my neighbors—in just one word, it would be: respect. The whole point of government is not to solve all of life's problems. Nor is it to settle every little disagreement among people. Instead, it should create an atmosphere where people can solve their own problems—without creating more problems for other people.

I am always reminded of the motto of the state of South Dakota: "Under God the People Rule." We, the people, believe in a smaller government—one that doesn't interfere with a person's ability to earn a living through hard work and innovation. One that respects each individual's rights.

No government can solve all of life's problems. No matter how well-intentioned some people might be, if they think the government can solve everyone's problems, all they are really doing is creating a big, wasteful bureaucratic mess that prevents people from solving their own problems, creates new problems, and pretty much leaves everybody miserable and mad at one another. Sound familiar?

So what is respect? As a child, my parents taught us that respect was minding our tongue, being disciplined in our behavior, and having manners.

Out on the ranch, a young child learned other aspects of the word "respect." We learned to respect the weather. The weather in South Dakota in the wintertime can literally kill you if you aren't prepared. A person needs to dress appropriately and prepare in case a sudden storm comes up and takes you by surprise and leaves you stranded. Respecting the weather didn't mean we were scared of it. It just meant that we learned as much as we could ahead of time and put the work into preparation that was necessary to deal with it.

We also learned a healthy respect for livestock. Our animals were part of our family and our business. For me in particular, they were also my friends. I was taught their behaviors, nutritional needs, natural tendencies. We learned the personalities of each. Respecting them meant caring about them in a way that acknowledged their dignity and unique characteristics as well as their value to our operation.

Later, when I had kids of my own, I found that interacting with and caring for animals was the best learning experience I could give them.

Booker, the youngest of our three children, was still quite young when I was elected to Congress. I had taught my daughters Kassidy and Kennedy how to care for their horses and practice for their horse shows and rodeos on their own during the week while I was away in DC. But Booker was only eight years old and just beginning to show horses when I started traveling so much. Kassidy, being the oldest at fifteen, would have to teach him most of the basics. Every week, I left them a list of drills and practice skills to go through in the arena while I was gone.

One day, I received a phone call from Kassidy, who was more than exasperated from dealing with Booker.

"Mom! What would you have done if I had sat on top of my horse in the middle of the arena and screamed at the top of my lungs that I didn't want to practice?" she asked.

"I would have gotten after you and not allowed it," I replied.

"Well, that's what Booker's doing right now!" she said, obviously at the end of her rope.

"What is Lexus doing?" I asked, curious about how the horse was handling this circus.

"She's just sitting there like a good horse," replied Kassidy.

"Go get your brother and put him on Skype right now."

A few minutes later, the screen on my desk in DC lit up with Booker's tear-streaked face.

"Booker, what on earth is going on?" I asked.

"Mom, I don't want to ride horses!" Huge tears rolled down his face, one by one.

"They make me itch, and Lexus goes *fast*, and Kassidy and Kennedy just yell at me all the time," he reported through his sobs.

"Were you screaming on Lexus's back?" I asked.

He sniffed before replying, "Yes."

"Booker, do you know what Lexus thinks when you scream like that?" I asked quietly.

He shook his head slowly and laid his head in his arms on the desk, crying silently, exhausted from all the drama of the afternoon.

"Booker, one of a horse's most dangerous enemies is a mountain lion," I said. "They attack horses by leaping down from trees onto their backs, using their claws to dig in so they can bite them in the neck and kill them. Horses fight with their teeth and their feet, but they can't defend their backs, and mountain lions are smart enough to know this. And horses are smart enough to know to never leave their backs unprotected. Their only defense in that situation is to run away. And Booker, did you know that mountain lions, when they roar, sound a lot like a human boy screaming? So when you're sitting on Lexus's back, and you're screaming, what do you think *she's* thinking?"

His head had risen up off his arms and he was listening intently to the story. His eyes got wide and he said, "She must have thought I was a mountain lion trying to eat her."

"What did she do?" I asked softly.

"She just stood there," he answered, thinking hard.

"Booker, look at how much Lexus must love you," I said. "Because even when she thought there could be a mountain lion attacking her, she knew she had to take care of you. She didn't run away. Instead, she stood there to make sure you were safe. Isn't she a wonderful horse to love you that much?"

His eyes started to tear up again and he nodded his head and wiped his nose on his sleeve. "I'm so sorry, Mama."

"Now, you go tell Lexus you are sorry. And you get on your horse, and you listen to your sister and practice hard. I will be home tomorrow, and we will talk about what went wrong today. Okay, bud?"

"Okay," he said.

Later that evening, I called Kassidy back.

"I don't know what all you said to Booker," she said, "but he went straight out to the arena, wrapped his arms around Lexus's front leg, and hugged her. He put his face in her chest and told her how sorry he was for acting that way."

Booker, Kassidy said, had been a perfect student the rest of the day.

Respecting animals means making the effort to understand them—their habits, needs, and even their fears. Respecting people often means taking those things into account too. None of us are perfect, but all of us deserve respect.

One of the most important aspects of respect is having the humility to realize you are not the only one with problems, and *you don't have all the answers to other people's problems*. This is something so many in our country seem to have forgotten—most especially in Washington, DC.

Another part of humility is respecting those who came before you by recognizing how much you benefit from decisions and sacrifices they made. Our parents often reminded us that we were blessed to inherit a family legacy. We heard stories of our ancestors and the hardships they sustained to establish their families, work the land, and put food on the table. Those stories were teaching moments for us generations later, and they gave us perspective. By comparison, whatever challenges we faced were actually not that hard at all, our parents told us.

"Your grandparents lived in a camper the first two years

they were married because they couldn't afford a house," Mom and Dad would often tell us. I remember hearing that story as a blizzard raged outside and we sat in our living room, toasty warm and protected from the elements. As often as I had heard it before, I understood it only in that moment.

Once, as my grandmother and I were putting away the dishes, she asked me if I knew why we always turned the drinking glasses upside down in the cupboard. I admitted that I had no idea. She said it was because of the "Dirty '30s"—when drought hit the prairie so hard and nothing would grow and the wind blew the soil into drifts like snow and blacked out the sun. The blowing dirt from the fields would even make its way into the houses. Even into kitchen cupboards. If the glasses weren't turned upside down, the next time you went to use one you would find it filled with dirt, my grandmother told me. So, they started to turn them upside down to keep the interior of the glass as clean as possible.

To this day we turn our glasses upside down—just out of habit from earlier generations.

These stories gave my siblings and me perspective. They also taught us lessons. One important lesson was that government can't solve all your problems any better than it could make the dust bowl go away or keep dirt out of your glasses. Another lesson was to "learn from the past so you don't repeat others' mistakes."

Chapter 5

No Herd Mentality

If I had to pick one thing that defined our life and my childhood, it would be farmwork. It did not matter how old you were, how big you were, whether you were a boy or a girl—if you were able-bodied, you were expected to pitch in. Our farm covered several thousand acres that Dad either owned or leased from relatives and neighbors for growing crops, so everybody had their share of chores.

Growing up on a farm, you don't have "helicopter parents." We learned by doing alongside our dad, or by the trial-and-error process of figuring it out ourselves until we got it right. The lessons I learned working for Dad on the farm are with me today.

Farm and ranch work is, of course, seasonal. Obviously, there was more time for extracurricular activities like playing basketball in the dead of winter, the time when there is the least to do outside on the farm. Yet, no matter the month, there was always something to be done. In the spring and summer, we were planting, cultivating, and fertilizing the crops and calving and branding the cattle. In the fall, we harvested and stored grain and reserved time for our annual cattle drive to bring the cattle home from pasture.

For us kids, work began the minute we stepped off the bus from school. The first thing we did was look to see if Dad was waiting in the yard. If he was, we knew we had exactly ten minutes to get changed out of our school clothes, grab a snack, and head outside to help with whatever he was doing.

If Dad wasn't in the yard—it was a completely different story! On those lucky days, we would stretch our ten-minute window to a glorious half hour. We would stroll into the house, dump our book bags, and click on the TV to watch *Captain 11* or *Gilligan's Island*. But one ear was always trained for the sound of a pickup driving into the yard or, heaven forbid, the front door slamming as Dad came looking for us. When this happened, we guiltily carried our bowls of Schwan's ice cream to the sink and hustled outside, knowing our reprieve had come to an end, and it was time to get to work.

And there was always plenty of work to do.

Few things have better prepared me for serving in public office than herding cattle. Successfully working with difficult personalities in tense situations to end up in a good spot is a skill I learned early in life, and it has certainly come in handy.

Calving season was always the most interesting. It began in mid-April. Every day—rain, shine, or snow—we rode out into the cow pastures to find any mothers that had given birth. We would round up the cow-calf pairs and move them across the road with the other pairs so we could keep a closer eye on them, protect them, and eventually begin the process of vaccinating and documenting the newborn calves into our herd.

Sometimes a cow needed help calving. When that happened, one lucky volunteer would insert an arm with a strap or chain inside the cow's womb and around the front hocks of the calf. The chain was attached to a "come-along" that was attached to the metal puller. When you cranked the come-along, and worked with the cow's contractions, the calf would usually slide out without too much trouble.

Most spring days, our after-school job was to take a couple of four-wheelers, a horse or two, and a pickup truck over to the calving pasture about a mile away from our house. This could be tricky business. New mama cows aren't too excited about humans on horseback or ATVs sidling up to their calves. If you have never faced an angry thousand-pound cow protecting her wobbly newborn calf, then you have missed out on some real fun. We always needed a strategy ahead of time—one that usually fell apart when the cows didn't follow the plan.

Often, cows kept their calves in hard-to-get-to places in the trees or in scrub brush on the other side of the creek. Usually our strategy was for one of us to ride up on a horse or four-wheeler and chase off the cow or, if the cow was being overly protective, get her to chase us. As soon as the cow and the calf were separated, the other person would run up, grab the calf, and tag it real quick before the mama realized what was going on. Once she did, she usually came back on a hard run. We'd have to get out of there—fast.

The most exciting day of the season always came whenever Green Tag #35 calved. "Green 35," as we called her, didn't cause us a lick of trouble all year long, but when she gave birth, she turned into the devil: she usually got a fever and became ornery. Her only goal then was to hurt anyone who got close to her calf.

Green 35 was a good mother, but she was smart, mean, and impossible to sneak up on. She always kept her calf in the most remote part of the pasture, usually lying out in the open, where there was no protection for anyone who dared approach them. To make things more interesting, her calves were always strong—and ready to run. Every year, when someone spotted that she had calved, they would get on the radio and announce: "Green 35's calved!" Everyone volunteered to come help move her and her calf. Really, they came to watch the show.

As soon as you pulled into the pasture, her head would fly up in the air, and she would start watching you from a mile away. This was not her first rodeo. She knew exactly what we were up to. If you approached on horseback or a four-wheeler, she would come charging after you once you got within a quarter mile of her and her calf. And she didn't stop. She would drop her head and go on a mission to teach you a lesson.

Cattle people always say you can kind of play with cows who charge because they close their eyes right before they hit you. Ordinarily, this gives you time to step aside—like some kind of South Dakotan matador. Not Green 35. She kept her eyes *open* the whole time so she could be sure she hit her target.

One year, my brothers and I just could not get Green 35's calf tagged. We had tried over and over again but to no avail. It was time for a new tactic. Rock and I were in the pickup truck across a ravine from her and her calf. Robb was on the four-wheeler closer to the cows on the other side of the creek. Our plan was fairly simple: Robb would try to get Green 35 to chase him the opposite direction from us. As soon as she left, Rock was to run down the muddy ravine, splash across the creek, grab her calf, and race back up the same way to jump into the bed of the truck. As the getaway driver, I would speed through the pasture and back across the road, hopefully with Green 35 chasing after us.

It was not how we normally moved cattle, but unique circumstances called for innovation and creativity. This seemed like a good plan to us, at least in theory.

Rock didn't usually work with the cows on an everyday basis like Robb and I did. He was often in the shop working

45

on equipment. But when we asked him to help us with Green 35, he was all in.

As planned, Robb got Green 35 to chase him, and he drew her away from her calf. Right on cue, Rock took off across the creek, snatched up the almost sixty-pound calf in his arms, and started back. As soon as he crossed the water, though, he got mired down in the mud. Watching from the pickup, I was getting nervous. By this point, Green 35 had noticed that Rock had grabbed her calf. She quit her pursuit of Robb on the four-wheeler, whipped around, started bellering, and lowered her head as she launched on a dead run straight for Rock, who was literally stuck in the mud.

"She's coming, Rock! *Run!*" I shouted.

Rock finally got clear of the mud and began to pick up speed, but Green 35 was closing fast. Rock tried to run faster, but the calf was fighting him and he wasn't making much headway. He wasn't going to make it to the pickup, and I couldn't get any closer to him because of the wet conditions. It was like watching a slow-motion train wreck.

By this time, Robb had turned the four-wheeler and was trying to catch up to intercept Green 35 before she could cross the creek and trample Rock. But the cow was moving too fast. As she ate up the ground between her and Rock, I changed my recommendation from "Run!" to *"Drop the calf! DROP THE CALF!"*

But Rock didn't drop the calf. He held on tight and kept running as fast as he could—which appeared to be not fast enough.

I shook my head at his determination to get that calf in the pickup or die trying. Personally, I was convinced he was a goner. The cow leaped the creek in one jump and kept coming, bellering death and destruction at my poor brother. As she closed in on Rock's heels, I watched helplessly from the pickup. Miraculously, Rock somehow found a fifth gear that kicked in like his life depended on it. Actually, it probably did.

Rock made it to the back of the pickup and rolled himself end over end with the calf wrapped in his arms tight to his chest. A split second later, Green 35 hit the back of the truck with her head—eyes wide open—charging so hard that the tailgate flew up and locked on its own. I hit the gas and gunned it.

We flew across the pasture for the road. Green 35 stayed right on our tail, blowing snot and bellering like she'd lost her mind. The truck went slightly airborne as we bumped across the gravel road and blew into the other pasture. I didn't even fully stop the truck before Rock leaned over the edge of the pickup and put the calf on the ground. The calf rolled once, jumped up, and his mom was right there, still huffing and snorting at us. She bellered one more time, shook her head, and the two of them turned and ran off over the hill—to the farthest corner they could get to.

I climbed out of the pickup just as Robb was pulling up on the four-wheeler. We both peered over the edge of the pickup box to check on Rock, who was lying there, gasping for air. Nobody said anything for a minute, until I broke the silence with a quiet question: "Why didn't you drop the calf?"

Rock looked at me in amazement. "It didn't even occur to me."

We burst out laughing.

There was an important lesson to be learned from Green 35 that afternoon: do not mess with angry moms!

To this day, I can't think of a cow we ever owned that was more dangerous. She was smart, sneaky, and determined to teach you a lesson. But as difficult as she was, she always had the healthiest calves, built right, who gained well. In the end, that's all that really mattered in a cattle operation like ours. So we kept her and her calving was always good entertainment.

Another afternoon during calving season, Robb drew the short straw. We were dealing with one more mean mother cow and needed to tag her calf and move them both into the calving pasture. We had already tried to use horses, but she kept knocking our horses around, and we didn't want them to get hurt. Since there were only two of us, our strategy was for Robb to get into the back of the pickup, and I would drive up next to the calf. Robb would jump out and grab the calf, pull it into the back end of the truck, and tag it. From there, we would get the cow to chase us across the road.

When I pulled up next to the calf, Robb jumped out, grabbed the calf, put it in the truck bed, and climbed in behind it. So far, so good. But the mama cow apparently was not on board with our plan. She came sprinting over to the truck, and when she got to us, she did not slow down. Instead, she jumped right into the back with Robb and her calf—all twelve hundred pounds of her! Robb dived over the side of the truck and hopped into the cab with me. I hit the gas and we took off across the pasture.

I crossed the road with a cow and a calf standing in the back of the pickup. When I finally stopped the truck in the field, our passenger cow looked around, a little puzzled. Then she and her calf jumped out and trotted off, happy as can be.

We never did manage to tag that calf. But we decided any cow willing to jump into the back end of a pickup just to protect her calf needed to be respected in a new way. Her calf would be just fine without an ear tag.

The horse I used most often was named Buddy. He was my sister Cindy's horse, trained by our neighbor and revered horseman Ky Adams. To this day, Buddy is legendary in our family. A 16-hand bay gelding that had no stop in him, Buddy gave you 110 percent every time. He was bred and trained for cutting cattle at ranch rodeos, but he was super handy in the pasture too. I don't think I truly appreciated just how smart he was, though, until one day we were moving pairs and one obstinate mother cow just kept charging our horses, over and over again. It was late in the day, and the horses were drenched in sweat and we weren't making any progress. I was just about to give up and give it a rest when this cow came charging toward Buddy again.

Before I knew what was happening, Buddy whipped around and kicked her with both hind feet square between the eyes. *Crack!* And just as quick, Buddy spun back around, lowered his head, and stood patiently watching. Hearing the sound, but not actually seeing what had taken place, I asked Robb, "What happened?"

"He kicked her! Both feet square between the eyes!" Robb replied, surprised. The cow was struggling to stay upright and stumbling around trying to get her bearings. Taking two steel horseshoes to the noggin had shaken her. Robb and I sat on our horses and watched, wondering if she was going to fall over dead. But after a few minutes she shook her head and trotted off with her calf, out the gate, over the road, and into the pasture, exactly where we wanted her to go.

Problem solved.

Chapter 6

Burning Daylight

John Wayne was a hero in our house. We all loved him (Mom loved him so much that her CB radio handle was "Duke"), and on the rare nights we had the chance to relax and sit down in front of the TV together, it was almost always to watch one of his movies. *Rio Bravo, Hondo, The Man Who Shot Liberty Valance*, and *Hatari!* were favorites. We would eat popcorn, dish up our ice cream—always Schwan's vanilla—and settle in for a night of fistfights, shoot-outs, and life lessons.

One of Dad's all-time favorite lines came from the John Wayne movie *The Cowboys*: "We're burning daylight!" Dad loved to use that line on us kids. And if we didn't hop to it, we might even get a boot to the backside.

John Wayne–style.

*   *   *

One day, Dad sent Robb and me over to the barn to try to get a calf to suck. Every time we climbed into the corral, the mama cow charged us, and we would have to retreat as fast as we could back over the fence. We tried outsmarting her and tricking her into the barn, with me opening the door and Robb ready to slam it shut after her. She stopped just short of the door each time and wheeled around to chase Robb through the corral instead. We tossed things at her. We tried grabbing her calf and dragging it inside. Nothing worked.

Defeated and out of ideas, we decided to go tell Dad we needed help. He was working in the shop that day because a recent rain had made it too wet to be in the field. He was busy welding together some parts when we walked in. We told him our dilemma. He just stared at us.

"I told you to get that cow in the barn and make the calf suck," he said plainly. "Don't come back until it's done. We're burning daylight."

Bewildered and tired, we went back to the barn and started all over again, but it was useless.

Again, heads hanging low, we returned slowly to the shop to tell Dad that the job he had given us was simply impossible. We knew he wouldn't be happy, but we had tried everything. The calf was getting weaker. The day was dragging on. We had no other option.

As soon as we walked into the shop, Dad could tell by the looks on our faces that we weren't able to get the job done. He just shook his head and dropped his tools. He pulled his rubber overshoes over his cowboy boots. His body language showed us that he was irritated at having to quit what he was doing to help us. He didn't even take time to buckle his overshoes, letting them flop open as he stomped to the barn and climbed over the fence.

Dad marched right up to the angry cow, waved his arm at her, and said, "Come on now! Git going!"

That cow shook her head back and forth, her eyes rolling back into their sockets as she blew snot out of her nose. Then she dropped her nose and pawed the ground. Her hoof flung mud and she breathed deeply, watching Dad. If you know cows at all, you know what happened next.

She charged.

I thought Dad was a goner. But he kept walking straight toward her. Crazy. When she reached him in the middle of the corral, Dad stretched out his arm and pushed her head to the side. He wrapped his arm around her neck and gripped her in a headlock. Then he began punching her giant black nose. Watching in disbelief from the top of the corral fence, Robb and I were stunned. Dad kept his grip on her and relentlessly twisted on her snout to try to direct her to the barn. His feet were braced out in front of him, trying to slow down her momentum as she bucked and bellered. We watched the two of them go around and around the corral. We'd never seen anything like this before. For Robb and me, it was shocking and, admittedly, a little entertaining— until Dad suddenly lost his footing and went down in the mud.

Finally free of Dad clinging to her neck, the cow turned on him. Dad was lying there on his back, and she dropped her head down onto his face and knelt down with her front knees directly on his chest. Next thing we knew, that cow was using her head to rub our father into the dirt and possibly out of this world.

Robb and I jumped off the fence like rodeo clowns and went to try to get the mad cow off of Dad. We ran at her to get her attention, which worked. She got up, charged at Robb, and chased him to the other side of the corral, where he leaped up and over the fence. Dad pulled himself out of the mud and hobbled to the fence, climbing up beside me.

Below, that cow looked from Robb to Dad to me. Then she turned and trotted across the corral and into the barn where her hungry calf was waiting. Apparently, she'd had enough.

Robb quickly slid down off the fence and shut the door behind her. Dad and I climbed down and met him in the middle of the corral. My brother and I glanced nervously at each other and then at Dad. What was he going to say about what had just unfolded? It was the first time in our lives we had ever seen a cow get the better of him. We watched as he first brushed himself off, then limped over to pick up his cowboy hat and brush it off.

Finally, Dad broke the silence. "Well, I had her right where I wanted her until I tripped on my overshoes," he said wearily.

We all started laughing.

Sure, you did, Dad, we thought. *Sure, you did.*

*　*　*

Growing up, I figured God must really love farmers. Just look at how often sowing and reaping are mentioned in the Bible! Over and over again the Good Book references barns overflowing, bringing in the harvest, and casting seed on fertile ground. It does take incredible faith to be in a profession where so much is out of your control.

One day when I was around fourteen years old, harvest was in full swing. As soon as I got home from basketball practice, I changed into my work clothes and hustled out to the shop to see where I was needed. When I came through the shop door, I could hear Dad over the radio, calling for an empty truck to be brought to the field. All the semis he had available to him were already filled to capacity and his combine was overflowing with grain. Harvest ground to a halt until someone brought another truck out. It just wasn't acceptable for the combine to be sitting idle.

Our shop manager, Craig, had just fixed the air brakes on a semi sitting in the shop. As he wiped the grease off his hands onto a dirty rag, Craig shouted, "Kristi! I'll open the overhead door. You back this truck out and run it out to your dad. Quick!"

I ran to the cab, pulled myself up and in, and started the engine. I waited for the pressure to build so I could release the brakes to back the rig out of the building. As the door went up behind me, I watched the gauges clear the necessary threshold. Then I released the brakes, shifted into reverse, let out the clutch, and goosed the engine. I backed the truck across the yard until I had cleared the buildings enough to make a wide turn and head down the driveway to the field.

As I came to a stop and started to shift into first gear, I realized that Craig was chasing me down, waving his arms to get me to stop. As he ran up to my window, I looked down at him with a questioning look. He was white as a sheet and simply said, "Your dad's pickup was behind the truck."

Dad had taken delivery the day before of a brand-new pickup. It was a wreck now.

When the door opened and I had rammed the semi into reverse, I didn't bother to check my side-view mirrors. I pushed that pickup truck all the way across the yard. Craig and I stood there in silence looking at the pickup. The entire side was smashed in, the tires were popped. It was obviously a total loss.

Finally, Craig turned to me and said, "Well, this truck needs to get to the field, and you need to go tell your dad what just happened to his pickup."

And he walked away.

I climbed back up into the semi and slowly drove to the field. I racked my brain trying to figure out how I was going to tell Dad what I had just done. When I got to the field, I parked the truck. I pulled back the tarp from the trailer so it could be loaded with grain and then waited for Dad to pull the combine beside it to unload his overflowing hopper. As he emptied the grain into the back of the semi, I climbed the ladder to the cab of the combine. I opened the door and sat down in the seat beside him.

There was no easy way to say it. I just needed to tell him what happened.

"I backed the semi out of the shop and your new pickup was parked there and I wrecked it," I told him.

He was quiet. This was unusual.

"How bad is it?" he asked.

"It's bad. I'm sure it's totaled. I'm sorry," I said.

He sat there, his jaw clenched, hands gripping the steering wheel, staring at me for a long time.

Finally, he said, "All right. Get out."

Dad never brought it up again. It was the only time in my life I remember not having to face consequences for something I had done wrong.

Better believe I check the side mirrors now.

When we worked with Dad, everything needed to be done right and quickly. When we were fixing fences with him, we learned to anticipate what tool he would need before he had to ask for it. I remember once while we were building a fence at the east ranch, he had to impatiently wait for me to run to the pickup and get the post driver for him.

When I got back from the truck with the tool, he was obviously disappointed that he'd had to wait for me to retrieve it. He looked at me and said, "Listen, you should know what I need before I know what I need!" I remember being shocked and bewildered by what that meant. How was I ever going to know what he needed before *he* knew what he needed?

That daylight was always burning. Seriously.

In hindsight, I realize he was teaching me to always be thinking three or four steps ahead. To be more efficient. To be proactive and solve a problem before it was a problem.

As a result of needing to get things done quickly, we often drove a little too fast when we were growing up. Our punishment was that we had to pay our own traffic tickets and then pay *Dad* the same amount as an extra level of financial pain.

When equipment broke down, it was normal for Dad to say, "Listen, you get to town and get those parts as fast as you can and get straight back here! Every minute that tractor sits, we lose money." We were just kids, but we didn't want to lose money. So we hurried to town and back (and everywhere else). If we happened to get pulled over and get a ticket, well, that wasn't great, but it was sure better than being slow. So when I got older, it just never really occurred to me that speeding tickets were a big deal. It wasn't a good thing, obviously. They did come with fines you had to pay. But it wasn't necessarily terrible. Much later in life, after I got into politics, those speeding habits would come back to bite me.

One hot fall day, perfect for harvesting, the combine broke down and Dad needed to run to town and get parts. Since we couldn't do anything in the field until it was fixed, Dad waved me over to the truck and said, "Hop in. Let's go get the parts quick."

The parts were all ready to go at John Deere and they were sitting on the counter. He scooped them up and headed right back out the door. We were several miles back down the road when we heard sirens behind us and looked in the mirror to see the flashing lights of a highway patrol vehicle, signaling for us to pull over.

Dad shook his head and pulled over on the shoulder of the road. He rolled down his window as the officer approached the vehicle.

"Good afternoon, sir. Can I see your license and registration, please?" asked the trooper.

Dad quickly said, "Listen, I'm in a hurry. The combine is broken down and I need to get it fixed and going again. If you want to write me a ticket, that's fine. But you will have to follow me to the field to do it because I need to get going."

To my complete amazement, the officer simply nodded in agreement. He got back into his cruiser and followed us back to the field and wrote out the speeding ticket while Dad lay under the combine replacing the broken part.

Obviously, that highway patrolman understood burning daylight.

I love this story because it shows what small-town America is like. My dad loved and respected law enforcement. He never argued over a ticket, always looked the officer directly in the eye and shook hands and thanked them for their service.

This police officer was a neighbor and a friend. He understood the immense amount of pressure my dad was under as well. He knew that farmers worked all year to grow a crop and then had a small window of time to get all of the mature crop in from the field and into storage before the snow started falling. Everything could be lost. A little understanding went a long way. And the lesson is that sometimes we just need to try to put ourselves in someone else's shoes for a bit and see things from their perspective.

Working on a farm was tough. But every day I thank the Lord for my upbringing. One of the best gifts my parents gave to us kids was assigning us seemingly impossible things to do. Life isn't easy and the road to success isn't always paved by someone else. It takes work and there are huge benefits to laying a few bricks yourself.

One example of this was that I was never "taught" to drive a semi. One day when I was twelve or thirteen, Dad and I were leaving the field with a full load of corn headed for home. I was sitting in the passenger seat. As we started rolling down the road, he suddenly remembered that he needed to bring another vehicle home too. So he turned to me and said, "Here, come take the wheel. Take the truck home."

His only advice: "Make your corners wide."

As I watched in disbelief, he jumped out of the truck and headed for the other vehicle.

I slid across the cab and grabbed the wheel. I told myself to stay calm. I could do this—even though I had driven many vehicles and tractors before, I had never driven a semi, and I didn't have a driver's license. On the farm we knew the basics of driving at a young age. But this was on a different level.

Somehow, I settled in and kept the semi going down the road. I drove the seven miles home without stopping or shifting gears—because I simply didn't know how to do that.

As I pulled into the yard, I turned the engine off and drifted to a stop before applying the air brakes. I had done it and lived to tell about it! Suddenly, I had become a semi driver. I felt a new level of confidence come over me. To this day, I distinctly remember the proud feeling that if I could drive an 18-wheeler, I could probably drive anything! The next time someone told me to jump in and drive a strange tractor or piece of equipment, I hopped in feeling assured that I could figure it out.

The older I get—and as I watch my own children grow into responsible, capable adults—I realize how that attitude made all the difference in the world for me. It made me more willing to try new things on and off the farm. It also taught me to fear nothing.

There is something very American about being self-taught and self-starting. We might not know everything when we embark on a new adventure or set out to conquer a new frontier. But we will figure it out along the way. The fear of the unknown is not an excuse to do nothing. It was those very experiences with my dad that taught me that.

This has been particularly important to me as governor of South Dakota during some pretty hard times. No matter how tough the situation, you cannot simply shut down or walk away or hide. You have no choice but to make the smartest decisions you can based on all the available information. If political opponents want to tear you up about it, so be it. Make a decision, stay the course, and be confident.

Growing up with a father like mine was challenging, exciting, exasperating, and inspiring. It forced all of us kids to be problem solvers. When Dad gave us a job, he expected it to be done. He didn't want us to come back to him with excuses or even valid "reasons" for why we didn't accomplish a task. He knew we could do it, so we did. Simple. I think too often government officials try to find a reason not to get things done. It's too hard, it's never been done before, or they are just lazy and want to make excuses. When you grow up the way we and millions of other Americans did, it's hard to understand why our government fails so many people.

One day when I was a young teenager, my dad came into the shop where I was working and said, "C'mon, Kris, I want to show you something."

We climbed into the pickup and headed east down the driveway. We drove several miles, right past Kones Korner, the local gas station and gun shop. I was disappointed when we didn't turn in. Curt, Vi, and Vic, the family owners, were some of my favorite people, and we were always guaranteed a can of pop or a snack. (Although Dad wouldn't allow us to roll dice with Vic for a free pop—that would be gambling, and we weren't allowed to gamble.) I knew better than to ask where we were going. Dad seemed to want this to be a surprise.

We pulled into a driveway, past the long grass, and up to a white farmhouse. Dad got out and opened some gates and then drove out across some rocky, hilly pastures—not a tree in sight. It was beautiful.

He came to a stop and climbed out. So I got out, too, and met him on the hill in front of the pickup. It had been too steep and too rocky to drive the pickup all the way up to the top. Looking over the landscape, he pulled out a dry tall stem of grass, stuck it between his teeth, and started to chew it. He glanced at me and asked, "What do you think?"

"It's beautiful," I said quietly, still gazing at the blowing grasses. The hills and terrain were very different from the land at our farm, even though we were only about fifteen miles away. "I love it," I said gently as I took it all in.

While I loved our farm where I grew up, this hilltop was wild and untouched. It felt more rugged—more *western*. My favorite things in the world at that time were the cows and horses. Standing there I could already picture our black Angus cattle scattered over the hillsides, calves frolicking and playing with one another. Nearby, I could already picture in my mind one mother cow lying among the calves, holding forth over day care for the afternoon.

Did you know cows do that? Look over at the next pasture you drive by on the highway and observe. If it is in the afternoon and the cattle are off grazing the hills, often you will find one area where the vast majority of the young calves will be playing, butting heads, or stretched out on their sides taking a nap. And right there among all the calves you will see a lone mama cow overseeing the whole crew. As a girl growing up on a farm, it always made perfect sense to me. It was just as if all the other moms had dropped the kids off at day care with one mama so they could go out for lunch and take a break for a bit before having to come back to collect their babies.

As my imagination got the better of me and I began thinking about how fun it would be to ride my horse across these acres of openness, I was jolted back to reality by my dad's voice.

"I just bought it," he said.

My head snapped around and I looked at him in surprise. "You bought it?"

"Yep," he said. "Just finalized the sale today. It's ours."

He went on to tell me how this land *was* different. It was what we call "native ground." It had never been turned or plowed. It had always looked like this. And it was hundreds and hundreds of acres in one piece, which is hard to find in our area of South Dakota.

Dad described how you could tell native soil by the grasses growing on it, how it lay against the horizon, and how there was this one little flower that grew only on native soil in South Dakota. It was called a pasqueflower, and you couldn't find it on tilled ground.

With its lavender leaves, the pasqueflower looks delicate all right, but in fact it is among the toughest flowers that exist. These are the first to bloom in the spring, often right next to a snowbank. They are hard to spot, though: you might almost step on one before you notice the little splash of purple poking out among the dead brown grass, a promise that spring has arrived and everything else will be blooming soon.

Dad told me the pasqueflower was our state's official flower because it most represented South Dakota and the toughness of our people.

"Can I live here someday?" I asked him.

He looked at me for a minute, then said bluntly, "You can buy it from me someday."

There was no free lunch in Dad's world.

Because of Dad's chronic back problems, a result of riding broncs in his younger years, compounded by literally back-breaking farmwork, pain radiated down his legs after a full day of work. Each night, one of us kids would walk on his back and legs, or rub his feet. Once you started, you were captive for the night, and we could never seem to rub hard enough or long enough to bring him complete relief.

I think now about how badly his body must have hurt to ask for help every night to get a little bit of relief so he could rest. It didn't matter what time I woke up or wandered downstairs in the middle of the night to get a drink of water—Dad was almost always awake. Usually, he would be reading his Bible in the living room or kneeling by a chair praying.

It wasn't until years later that I realized he was always awake because he was in too much pain to sleep. The only time I ever really saw his face relaxed was when he would doze off on the couch after a good foot rub.

I feel guilty now for the complaining I did to get out of that particular chore, one that brought him even the tiniest bit of relief. This may sound strange, but I'd give anything to rub his feet for him one more time. I remember those times now as precious memories where Dad and I would talk, share a laugh at a funny joke on the TV, or talk about school, work, or basketball. At the time, of course, I was focused on the work of it—not the blessing of it. Now that blessing is gone.

It's odd how something I was just trying to get through became a memory that I cherish. It seemed like a chore at the time, but really it was a gift. That's a lesson I've kept with me all the years since. It can be so easy to take them for granted, but daylight is burning with the people we love too.

Chapter 7

Love Is Patient

Bryon Noem and I attended the same high school, although we didn't start dating until I was a junior. He is two years older than me and was friends with my brother Rock. But since we all went to such a small school, everybody knew one another.

Bryon grew up on a farm just about ten miles southeast of ours, the second of three boys born to Al and Sharon Noem. Their family worked hard together raising crops, hogs, and cattle. The three brothers also played a lot of sports. Bryon was the quarterback of the high school football team, started for the varsity basketball team, ran track, and played baseball in the summers. After he graduated, Bryon went off to college at Northern State University to play football and pitch for the baseball team.

At that time, a friend of mine was dating Bryon's cousin, and I let her know that I thought Bryon was pretty special.

So they worked together to get Bryon to return for homecoming. I was a cheerleader for the football team, and I saw him right away in the crowd when he got to the game. After, we all went to the homecoming dance, but he never asked me to dance. He didn't even talk to me! I was so disappointed, and I just assumed he wasn't interested.

Two weeks later, Bryon showed up for the next home game, where I was cheerleading as usual. Afterward, everybody went to the bowling alley. We ate pizza, talked, and hung out for a while. But again, Bryon never even approached me to start a conversation. He was too busy talking to his friends. Confused as to why he would drive two hours to come back for the game if he wasn't even going to talk to me, I decided to head home for the night.

Driving home, I could not help but notice a strange car following me. In a lot of places, this might not seem like a big deal. But where we lived, there just were not that many cars. As the miles went by and I got closer to home, the car closed the distance between us.

Okay, I thought. *This is getting very strange.*

When I finally turned the corner for the mile-long drive into our yard, I realized that I recognized the car. The car turned to follow me and flashed its lights. I pulled over and the car stopped behind me. A tall man got out.

Normally, I might have been freaked out by the whole situation. Not now.

Bryon leaned down and knocked on my window.

"Hi. I was just wondering if we could talk for a while?"

It was about time!

"Get in," I said.

We sat there on that calm, starlit night parked alongside the driveway to our farm and we talked for several hours—about school, the game, and our families. After a while, Bryon got back into his car and drove home.

I thought for sure I'd hear from him in a day or two. *Weeks* went by before, finally, he called. And then it would still be several months more before he would talk to me in public. He preferred his follow-me-home routine. We would be out together at the same football game. I would head home. He would follow me. And then we would sit in my car in front of my house and talk for hours—sometimes until three or four in the morning.

I was always surprised my mom and dad would allow it, actually. One night my mom came out to the car with a flashlight to "check on us."

She later told me that when she and Dad would go to bed each night, Dad would ask, "Is Kristi home?"

"Yes," Mom would answer. "She and Bryon are sitting out front."

Dad would always ask, "Are they sitting up?"

We always were, of course. We weren't dummies.

Bryon and I got engaged on the Fourth of July, 1991.

I was a 4-H leader at the time, and I had agreed to take my 4-H kids to participate in the parade in Watertown. It was a hot day and many of my 4-H families had plans to go to the lake on the Fourth instead of standing on a hot, miserable sidewalk watching their kids trot by on horses. Since I had a big horse trailer, I offered to just take their kids to the parade for them. It turned into a major ordeal.

I ended up picking up kids and horses from five or six different homes. Then I rounded up another eight to ten kids who met us at the parade—all with their horses. I helped get them all saddled up and polished. The horses had to be brushed. The kids needed to be in their club vests. I was—literally—the only adult riding with them in the parade. You could say it was stressful.

Making matters even more interesting were all the distractions for the cavalry of twenty-five horses ridden by children that I was leading down the parade route. Fire trucks, clowns, and all sorts of loud noises. One sudden move or sound and all the horses could spook, carrying kids off with them. I seriously questioned my sanity in thinking this would be a good idea.

Luckily, Bryon came to watch the parade. But since he knew very little about horses, he was limited in how much he could help. Afterward, I unsaddled the horses, loaded up the kids, and delivered them all home again. At the end of the day, I was exhausted.

Bryon had wanted to go out to dinner that night and then take his grandpa's boat out on the lake to watch the city fireworks. But as I unloaded my horse back home and unhooked the trailer, I decided I was too tired and dirty to go anywhere. I went inside to call him and cancel before taking a shower.

When I told him I just wanted to stay home, he would have none of it. He *insisted* on taking me to dinner. Dusty, drained, and exhausted, I reluctantly agreed. I got in the shower and started to clean up.

I was in a pretty sour mood by the time Bryon picked me up. I was not very talkative. When I did talk, it was about everything that had gone wrong that day. Bryon listened quietly. As we sat down to dinner, he told me he had gotten his grandpa's boat and put it in the water. It was ready for us to go out and watch fireworks after we finished eating.

At this point, I was all out of patience. I told him I simply was *not* going out in his grandpa's boat with him. I wasn't interested in watching fireworks. And I certainly wasn't interested in going out in a boat in the *dark*. Anyway, I had forgotten my jacket. The matter was settled.

Instead, Bryon Noem looked at me across the table and said very calmly: "I don't care what you say. We are going."

We finished our dinner and went out to the truck in silence. As we drove to the lake, he kept trying to start a conversation. But I would have none of it. I was angry, and I was not going to make it easy on him.

When we climbed into the boat, I was still sulking. He motored us out into the middle of the lake, where we waited for the show to begin. As the fireworks began, I was cold and miserable. I went to get the blanket from the front of the boat.

As I turned around, Bryon was bent down for some reason.

He was kneeling.

On one knee.

In his hand, he held a ring and he was looking up at me.

"Kristi, will you marry me?" he asked as we bobbed around on the dark, cold lake as fireworks exploded overhead.

I was shocked. I just stared at him. In silence. Finally, I blurted out the only thing that popped into my head, knowing it was a mandatory in our family.

"Did...you ask my dad?"

"Yes, I asked your dad," he replied, clearly annoyed.

"What did he say?"

"He said yes—if *you* said yes."

"Okay, yes!" I said. "I will marry you!"

Less than a year later, we got married during one of the coldest, wettest springs South Dakota had seen in years. In May 1992, it rained for weeks and no one in the area had been in the field yet to plant any crops. That was unprecedented. Every farmer was stressed knowing that every day lost putting seed in the ground was another day of the growing season lost. And that meant their yields would be cut. They were losing money by the day.

Things were even worse for my dad, who had been bedridden for months with excruciating back pain. I had been helping him more and more, but he still had to hire additional help on the farm. On top of all that, he was having to pay for his second wedding in less than a year. He had lost a lot of weight and I was not even sure he would be able to walk me down the aisle.

He did.

After the ceremony, we hired a horse and buggy to take us from the church several miles to an outdoor reception at my grandparents' acreage. It was chilly weather, but a fun day and Dad made it through.

Bryon had never traveled outside of the state before except for one trip to Minneapolis with his family, so planning our honeymoon was an adventure. And like so many newly married couples, we were on a tight budget. I mean *really* tight. We had many discussions about whether we "needed" something or just "wanted" it. To spend money on a trip was a huge decision. For months before the wedding we discussed various options.

I finally asked him, "If you could go anywhere in the world, where would you go?"

Bryon thought about it for a minute. "Dodger Stadium," he said. He was a lifelong Dodger fan and had grown up watching their games with his dad and brothers.

"Then let's go to Dodger Stadium."

For the first time, he got really excited to make a honeymoon plan.

The problem was, the Dodgers did not play at Dodger Stadium the week after our wedding. They were on the road. It was not until two weeks later that they played back in Los Angeles. So we got married on Saturday and stayed at a hotel one night and then went home. But the little farmhouse we lived in at the time was pretty empty. We didn't have furniture. Or a television. Or a radio. We *did* have a record player, but only a handful of records. By Sunday night, we were pretty bored and decided to drive to the farm and visit my family. Boy, were they surprised to see the newlyweds walk in the door just twenty-four hours after getting married! We got up early the next day and went right to work on the farm, just like usual.

Once the weekend finally arrived, we caught a plane for Los Angeles to go to Dodger Stadium to watch the Dodgers play baseball.

I will admit, I was not the world's biggest baseball fan when we got married. So I was not fully prepared for what a honeymoon at a Major League Baseball stadium would look like.

For starters, the hotel was advertised as being on the beach. It was not. The beach was five miles away. When we got there to check in, they informed us that the rate would be $105 a night—more than we had been led to believe. On top of that, we would be charged another $5 a day for parking our rental car. All of which meant we spent a good part of every day driving around Los Angeles in search of a cheaper hotel and free parking.

We never did find any.

All that driving around, however, did not exactly broaden

our dining options. We ate every meal at either Dodger Stadium or McDonald's. Because my husband was frugal, and we had no money, I was limited to one Diet Coke a day.

As for the beach that our room supposedly overlooked? We spent a total of one hour on it the entire trip. And, again, that was five miles away from our hotel.

The highlight, of course, was the stadium itself. At least it was for Bryon, who had borrowed my dad's video camera to capture *every* detail. To this day, the entirety of our honeymoon video collection consists of eleven hours of footage from inside Dodger Stadium.

Not that we were allowed to bring a video camera inside. We weren't. But try telling that to Bryon. No stadium rules were going to keep him from recording our honeymoon. And it didn't matter to him that the camera was the size of a suitcase and bright yellow—in other words, impossible to casually smuggle inside and around the stadium.

And you better believe we were not going to miss batting practice.

Once Bryon got us settled in our seats, he disappeared to film different parts of the stadium before the game started. It was fun watching him across the stadium, with his giant, bright yellow camera, filming everything—while being chased by security guards. Eventually, they caught him and made him take the camera out to the car before the game started.

Oh, there was another thing I did not realize about spending your honeymoon at Dodger Stadium. Turns out, you don't fly all the way out to Los Angeles to watch just one game at Dodger Stadium. You go out there to watch the *entire series* of games going on that week at Dodger Stadium.

Four full days of baseball and Bryon was going to get every penny's and every minute's worth.

As annoying as that camera may have been on our honeymoon, our family has hours of home videos of the kids growing up (long before smartphones, mind you) because Bryon took the time to capture those moments. That is my husband in a nutshell: He never loses sight of the present moment. He has never missed what is most important. Bryon is also the one in our family who reminds us to enjoy life, to slow down, not work so hard, and make memories.

Bryon loves to surprise me. Every year, he throws me a surprise birthday party and calls up friends, family, colleagues, and staff for what's usually a pretty large and covert operation. There's just one problem: I *hate* surprises. Simply can't stand them. And every one of our family, friends, colleagues, and staff knows this about me. Without fail, they try to dissuade Bryon from whatever plan he's got, and every year he just pushes right ahead. Invariably, I show up dressed way too casually for the extravaganza, and all the guests are anxious because they know my feelings about surprises, but Bryon's there just loving it.

The truth is, God gave me a husband perfectly suited for

me. I'm task-oriented; Bryon is *people*-oriented. He's more attuned to the emotional needs of others than I am. He often points out how direct I am in the way I speak, explaining how that can make people *feel*. On money, Bryon deliberates over big purchasing decisions, again the perfect balance for me, because I'm prone to making decisions quickly.

All through our marriage, Bryon has never seen any job as "my job" or "his job." He has pitched in everywhere— inside the house, outside the house, caring for the children. He saw everything as much his priority as mine. He coached the kids' sporting events, he signed up to lead at Bible camps, and he helped me teach Sunday school, Vacation Bible School, and any other activity where he saw a need.

Bryon prays. Plenty of people do, but Bryon allows prayer to change his life—he acts on the prompts he gets. There's one particular example of this I will share more about later— one that changed our family dramatically and forever—but it has been a hallmark of my husband's life and of our marriage. And I am incredibly grateful for him.

First Corinthians 13:4–8 is a well-known passage, often used at weddings, and there's a saying that if you can substitute the name of your potential spouse for the word "love," you know you have someone worth holding on to forever. The passage goes like this:

Love is patient, love is kind. It does not envy, it does not boast, it is not proud. It does not dishonor others, it is not self-seeking, it is not easily angered, it keeps no record of wrongs. Love does not delight in evil but rejoices with the truth. It always protects, always trusts, always hopes, always perseveres. Love never fails. (NIV)

Bryon's name fits.

Chapter 8

The Day We Lost Him

Bryon had just walked in the door and answered the phone in the kitchen. I was making supper. I remember that Bryon had hurried home because we needed to get to town for childbirth classes that night in Watertown. At twenty-two, I was eight months pregnant with our first child.

It was Joanie Butala on the phone, a forever family friend, who was also the secretary for the farm. She did all the books for our farm businesses and always had her finger on the pulse of the daily goings-on.

"I need to speak to Kristi," Joanie told Bryon. He could sense the tension in her voice.

What made her phone call that cold March evening a little strange was that—for the first time in my life—I *wasn't* working for my father. Three or four months earlier, Dad and I had gotten into an argument. Looking back today, the fight seems pretty stupid. At the time, it was a big deal to me. Probably to him too.

The real problem was that we were both so very much alike. We were both very exacting, very particular about how things needed to be done. And we were both very headstrong. Most importantly, we both wanted to be in charge.

I was frustrated that it seemed I could never do anything right for him. He was always telling me what to do, when to do it, and how he wanted me to do it, which of course was what parents did. He was never going to stop being the boss, but I was growing up and anxious to take on more responsibility.

In 1994, I was twenty-two years old, married, pregnant, and I felt I was ready to be in charge. One morning, Dad and I had an argument over how I fed the cows and how I had left a bag of mineral by the gate so I could use it later that afternoon. He wanted everything put away in the shed all the time, even though the bag was going to be sitting there for only two to three hours. He felt it was lazy of me not to put it away. I felt it was a waste of time to take it all the way across the yard and put it away when I was going to have to go get it again right after lunch.

Like I said, this argument was really stupid. But he just would not let it go, and—of course—I refused to back down from doing it my way. The whole discussion spilled over into lunch in the kitchen and he was still talking to me about it.

Finally, I told him, "I can't take it anymore. I can't do anything right for you."

"Fine," he said. "Find yourself a job somewhere working for somebody else who lets you do anything you want."

Truth is, he was my dad and I loved him very much. Instead of working for him, I just wanted to love him. But I was frustrated and impatient and stubborn. And so was he. So I quit.

For the first time in my life, I wasn't working on the farm. I went to town and got a job at a vacuum cleaner store, selling carpet-cleaning services over the phone. It was a fine job working for really wonderful people. But it was not what the girl who had spent her entire life dreaming of farming and ranching wanted to be doing.

Anyway, on that particular March day when Joanie called, Bryon had been working on the farm for Dad. I had spent the day making calls at the vacuum cleaner store. So when Joanie called the house, I thought it was a little strange that she wanted to talk to me since I was no longer employed at the farm. Puzzled, I walked across the kitchen and Bryon handed me the phone.

"Hi, Joanie, what's up?"

Even though Dad and I had that argument and even though I'd quit working for him on the farm, we still talked and visited a lot. I guess maybe quitting and not working for him had kind of helped. Things were easier between us. Since I wasn't under his thumb all the time anymore, I really could focus more on loving him and looking out for him.

I remember when I was five or six months pregnant Dad asked me if I wanted to go deer hunting in the Black Hills with him for a few days. I had left working on the farm and thought it would be a great trip and an opportunity to spend time with him. What made the trip even more exciting was that we were going on horseback. Of course, Bryon and Mom were worried about me being away and so far along in the pregnancy. As they both argued why I shouldn't go, Dad just said, "She'll be fine."

What I loved about the trip was that while my life was changing, and my body was changing, and everyone was treating me like I was broken, my dad was treating me like he always did—like I was *tough*. Like I could do anything. I appreciated how he helped me feel normal when so many things about being a new wife and soon-to-be mom were totally not normal for me.

The day before Joanie called the house was a Wednesday. I remember that because Wednesday nights we had church and if the doors were open, Dad was there. And so was I.

After the service, we would all typically go to the Millstone Family Restaurant for coffee and pie. But that night I was tired. I was pregnant and had worked all day at the vacuum store and just wanted to get some rest.

I remember telling my dad in the church parking lot how Bryon and I had just finished fixing up the nursery in our house. He was engaged and asked lots of questions about it. I thought it was sweet of him to be so interested. So I invited him to come over and see the nursery on his way home from church. He told us he would after stopping at the restaurant.

It was all very kind, and stood out to me because Dad was not the kind of guy who took the time for such things. The idea that he would even be talking about a baby nursery was kind of remarkable. The idea that he would pay a special visit just to see the nursery was borderline strange. But he was really excited about the baby. It was, after all, his first grandchild.

Like I said, I guess less fighting was leading to us just showing that we cared about each other more—and that was a good thing.

Anyway, he called later that evening to ask if it was okay if he didn't stop by to see the nursery that night. He was exhausted after a long day of working and then church. He had an early day the next day, too, but he promised he would come see it soon—before the baby was born.

To this day, I am still sad he was not able to stop by, but I certainly understood. As I hung up the phone, I mainly just appreciated his thoughtfulness about all of it. It was a side of Dad he rarely had time to show me.

What I didn't know as I hung up the phone that night was that it would be the last time I would ever hear my dad's voice while he was alive. Looking back, sometimes it's the small things we remember the most but don't recognize their importance at the time. I had no idea that phone call, and his earlier questions about the nursery, would be some of the last memories of my father. But they showed just how much he loved his family and the thought of his new grandbaby.

It had been a warmer than usual spring. Even though it was still March, temperatures outside were getting up to 50 or even 60 degrees. It would drop below freezing at night, but then warm up during the day. That kind of weather might not be an issue if you are working at Target, but it wreaks all kinds of havoc on stored grain. Especially high-moisture grain like the kind Dad had.

Our farm had several fifty-thousand-bushel grain bins. Each one held fifty semi-loads of grain. They were those giant round things you see from the airplane window when you fly over farm country, and few things on a farm are more important. Depending on the price of grain that year, a farmer has a small fortune stored in each one. They are where the fruit of a farmer's labors are stored at the end of a growing season.

Each grain bin is two or three stories tall, with metal sides and a ladder running up to a hatch on the top. At the bottom is a machine called an auger. It is basically a giant screw that rotates and turns so that the blade pushes corn upward through a pipe to be loaded into a trailer and hauled to market or processed into livestock feed.

Adding to the misery of that year's grain situation was that the previous growing season had not been great because of how much rain we'd had. All that autumn rain meant the corn had a high moisture content when it was harvested.

The grain bins are equipped with fans to circulate air to help draw off the moisture as the corn dries, but they can do only so much. Come the following spring, the corn was still volatile. Add in the fluctuating temperatures and you get what's known as "hot" corn: the corn freezes and thaws and holds on to all that moisture. Then it begins to ferment, eventually growing a crusty mold across the top. This crust, in turn, makes it harder to circulate fresh, dry air throughout the rest of the bin to dry the grain underneath.

Making matters even worse is that the crust creates cavities, like pockets, under the surface when any amount of grain is removed. The mold prevents the loose kernels of corn from falling to the floor so the auger can pull it up. So not only do you have lousy corn, but you can't get rid of it. It is a constant chore under those conditions to keep the grain loose and the air circulating. The only reliable way to do that is to climb up the side of the bin, open the hatch, and climb in to break up the crust with your feet or maybe a shovel.

On this particular day, my brother Robb, who was a senior in high school, came home from a day in the classroom and had been working in the shop. Dad asked him to help pull a semi-load out of the middle grain bin because it was getting hot. Dad wanted to then break up the crust on top in hopes of that helping the corn dry.

Robb was ready to go in the house, but, of course, he agreed. He pulled the grain cart around and parked it underneath the auger. He switched it on to begin pulling grain out of the bottom of the bin into the trailer.

Typically, the auger pulls grain from the center before sucking up corn from the edges. Robb climbed up the ladder and swung his leg into the bin and was about to step onto the crust to break it up as the corn began to empty from the bottom. Suddenly, he heard Dad holler from below.

"Hey, let me get up there," he said. "I'll get in there and do that."

"I'm already up here," Robb replied. "I'll just do it."

Dad insisted. "No, let me do it. My back feels good today. It hasn't felt this good in months."

Robb just shook his head and climbed down.

Dad climbed the ladder and disappeared into the top of the bin to begin breaking up the crust. Robb decided to climb back up the bin and help since there really wasn't anything he could do while the truck filled. As soon as Robb got halfway up the ladder, he heard Dad shout: "Shut the auger off! Shut the auger off!"

Robb had no idea what had happened, but he jumped to the ground as fast as he could to unplug the auger then scrambled back up the ladder to the open hatch. He looked inside.

Dad was gone. All Robb could see was corn.

Apparently, Dad had punched through the crust and gotten sucked into a pocket underneath. The deadly thing about it was that falling through the crust had loosened all the corn. It had caved in on top of him. Dad was buried alive underneath tons of cold, damp corn.

But how deep was he? Where was he? Realizing the

enormity of what was happening immediately, Robb called out to him and thought he heard something coming from below the surface. Helpless and fearing the worst, Robb leaped down and raced as fast as he could to the shop across the yard, looking for help. Craig Wendling, one of the farm's longtime employees, was still at the shop working.

"Craig!" Robb called, breathless. "Dad got buried in the corn! He's stuck, and the corn caved in on him!"

Craig instantly knew what a dire emergency it was. Falling through crusty corn is worse than falling through ice on a lake in the winter. You cannot swim in corn and it will drown you just as fast as water. And then, depending on how far you fall into wet grain, the sheer weight of corn collapsing on top of you is enough to kill a man.

Craig picked up the phone. In those days, we still did not have 9-1-1 in rural South Dakota. You called your neighbors. Craig called the house and got Mom.

"Ron is buried in the corn," he told her. "Get help!" He hung up and ran out to the grain bin.

Mom started calling neighbors in Hazel, two miles away. She called the café first, but nobody answered. Then she called the grocery store. Still, nobody answered. It was already past five o'clock and most of the businesses had closed.

Her next call was to the grain elevator where farmers hauled their grain to sell. The man who manages the elevator answered. Mom told him what had happened. He told her there were several farmers there and they would all come right away. It must have been a crazy scene with all those trucks speeding out of the elevator yard headed south toward the farm.

I later learned that when Craig called her from the shop, my mom could not make out exactly what he said. She did not know if he had said, "Ron is buried in the corn," or "Robb is buried in the corn." So as she paced the house in the most terrifying moments of her life, she had no idea if it was her husband or her son who was lost in the grain bin behind the house, suffocating under tons of corn. That's when she called Joanie Butala, who had already gone home for the day.

As all this was unfolding, Bryon and I were still at home, getting ready for dinner and child birthing class. When Joanie called, she was all business and spoke urgently.

"Kristi, your dad is stuck in a bin and you need to come right away," she told me.

My first thought was, *I don't even want to know what that means.*

"Okay. He is stuck in a bin?" I asked.

"Yes," she said. "And you need to come right away."

My mind reeled as I considered the full range of what that could possibly mean for Dad.

This was not my dad's first encounter with augers and bins—one of the more serious dangers on a farm. We were always warned about how dangerous augers were, especially climbing into a bin full of grain. It was not a big surprise that Dad would take a risk like he did that day in the grain bin. It was also not a surprise that he insisted he go in there instead of Robb. While I did not know exactly what Joanie meant when she said he was "stuck in a bin," I assumed the worst.

Suddenly, everything slowed down. My farm-raised instincts kicked in. "Turn the fans on in the bin and I'll be right there," I told Joanie.

Bryon and I grabbed our coats and headed out the door to the truck. If Dad was stuck in the bin, or buried under grain, he would need fresh air. The fans were the only thing I could think of.

Robb and Craig had climbed into the bin after Dad with shovels. Desperately, they dug through the corn, reaching down into the yellow sea of grain for any sign of life. But it was hopeless. The space left by every shovelful of corn they dug out immediately filled back in with more corn. For all they knew, they were only making matters worse. Somehow, they needed to find him, and the only way to find him was to empty out the corn.

The one thing they could not do was the only sure way to empty the bin as fast as possible—turn on the auger. Because they had no idea where Dad was, they couldn't risk turning it on. As horrible as the whole situation was, the one thing that would make it so much worse was turning on the auger. If that auger blade nicked any part of his body, it would suck his whole body in, wrap it around the turning shaft, and tear him to pieces.

That's when Robb and Craig decided the best course of action was to just rip the whole bin apart. Craig jumped into the payloader, used the forks to pierce the side of the bin and grip the metal siding, and peeled it off as corn spilled out onto the frozen ground. As they worked, pickup trucks and vehicles began arriving at the farm in a cloud of dust. Help had arrived.

Two of the first people on the scene were Lyman Hanson, the grain elevator manager Mom had spoken to on the phone, and a high school classmate of mine, Ron Holiday. They immediately climbed into the bin and started digging as the payloader continued peeling back the sides of the bin. More volunteer firemen and neighbors arrived and joined in the search.

Ron was one of the first people to find Dad. He called out for help and everybody joined him in frantically digging corn away from Dad's face to give him air. At first, they could not determine if he had a pulse or was still breathing. But they could tell he was very cold. The heavy, wet corn was packed so tightly around him they could not pull him free.

They kept digging.

They began CPR as soon as they cleared the corn down to his chest. But they still could not pull him free. Even when they dug the corn all the way down to his knees, they couldn't free him from the grain.

In all, it took them almost forty-five minutes to find Dad and free his body. By then, an ambulance had arrived from

more than twenty miles away. The EMTs continued to per-
form CPR on him as well as other lifesaving measures as
they wheeled him into the ambulance.

Bryon and I got there as fast as we could. As we came down
the driveway into the farm, I remember there were trucks
everywhere, parked in the road and the yard, on the grass—
everywhere. And there were people everywhere.

As we got closer, I could see the bin had been torn apart
like a tin can twisted in half. Corn covered the ground
around it. The ambulance was just leaving with Dad, so we
kept driving past all the wreckage up to the house to check
on Mom.

By the time we got to the hospital, a lot of people in Watertown, where we attended church, had heard about the accident
and gathered. Someone had started calling neighbors, another
person called the prayer chain at church, and the news spread
like wildfire. I remember walking into the emergency entrance
and the waiting area was already packed with people from our
church, community, and farms all around ours. There were
too many to count, and I could not figure out how they had
gotten there before us. My dad's brothers and his mom were
already there waiting for an update on his condition. I was
quiet and didn't want to talk. I didn't want to ask questions
because I felt sure that I was not ready to hear the answers.

The emergency room staff took our small group to a private room just for family members. They told us they were working on Dad. The accident had happened just after five in the afternoon. We didn't get to the hospital until around six thirty. The doctors and nurses came in and out of the room, giving us updates.

"We're trying to get his body warmed up," they told us. "We think then we can get his heart started again and that maybe the cold kept him from suffering too much brain damage from the lack of oxygen."

It was all so bleak.

"And?" was all we could reply to the doctor. We looked at him, scanning his face for any signs of hope.

"Just pray," he said. And we did.

Over the hours, the doctors did manage to warm him up. Miraculously, they were able to get a heartbeat back. But they could not get any blood pressure. At one point, doctors cracked open his chest and began massaging his heart. All night, doctors kept coming back to give us updates, tears in their eyes.

Looking back, I realize that those doctors probably knew that he was dead for hours. But they never stopped working on him. They never let us give up hope. They never stopped telling us to pray. They never quit on our family and what we asked them to do. And they never quit on him. It still amazes me today how hard they worked to revive him.

As distraught as we all were, it was truly gratifying to see the number of people who showed up at the hospital that night. It seemed there were hundreds of people there. The emergency room was so packed that there were people outside in the parking lot who couldn't get in the doors at the hospital. It was shoulder to shoulder with people standing in silence and hoping for good news...and praying.

We waited in the small family room with Mom, Robb, my grandma, and Dad's siblings. Finally, near midnight, one of the doctors came in and knelt down in front of Mom and held her hands. He looked into her eyes as tears started to form in his own and said, "He's gone, Corinne. We need to let him go."

She dropped her head into their folded hands in her lap and started to sob. The rest of the room fell apart as well. I could literally feel the whole world shattering, and I knew we would never be the same.

All my life, Dad was invincible. Nothing could hurt him. He was unstoppable. It all just seemed so unbelievable to me. It couldn't possibly be true.

I was eight months pregnant, sitting in the same hospital where I was supposed to have attended childbirth classes that very same evening, preparing for a new life to enter the world. Instead, I was two floors down in the emergency room grieving for a life I didn't think could ever be lost.

After a few moments, everyone turned their worried eyes on me. They thought I was going to go into labor right then and there and have this baby. To be honest, their concern annoyed me. I knew the baby was fine. She had been kicking me all night, reminding me she was there, anxious to be out in the world. I just wanted to focus on the real problem: What are we going to do without the man most of our lives revolved around? How are we going to know what work needs to be done tomorrow, the next day, or for that matter, the rest of our lives?!

The doctors asked if we wanted to go see Dad's body. At first, I did not want to go, but then I thought I probably should. I remember thinking that if I did not actually see his body with my own eyes, I would never believe he was really dead.

I was one of the very first to go in. When I got there, I saw blood seeping from the corner of his mouth and I was instantly upset that they hadn't wiped that blood away. What if Mom had seen him with blood running out of his mouth? I grabbed a cloth and wiped his face before Mom came in to say goodbye.

It was after a moment of standing there, looking at him in disbelief, that I saw blood beginning to pool at the corner of his mouth again. I realized it wasn't going to stop, no doubt because of the trauma his body had gone through. It hadn't been the nurses' fault. Honestly, I had no idea who to blame for this horrible night.

It was long after midnight when we finally left the hospital and drove home. I remember not being able to talk and not being able to think as we drove through the darkness. We went back to Mom and Dad's house at the farm and decided to stay there for the night. We were too exhausted to go back to our house and I did not want to leave Mom alone. She had a friend who was staying with her, too, which was a relief for me. I didn't know how to console her. My sister, Cindy, would be better at that, but she was living in Georgia. I couldn't imagine what it was like for her and Rock, who was in Oklahoma, to get that phone call from our uncle telling them the news. Hours waiting to see if he was going to be okay and then getting the final call that Dad had died. I suddenly missed my brother and sister more than I ever thought possible. My siblings were the only ones who knew exactly how I was feeling. I realized it was probably much worse for Robb. He had been there the whole time and would live forever with those memories. One day I would ask him about what all happened...but not tonight. Not anytime soon.

Bryon and I went upstairs to sleep in my childhood bedroom. It was strange how everybody just came home and said good night and went up to bed, like it was a normal night. Like our world had not just turned upside down.

I lay down in bed next to Bryon and he fell asleep right away. It was one or two o'clock in the morning, but for some reason I was angry that he just fell asleep like that.

I remember lying there in bed—awake all night long—staring at the ceiling and wondering what we were ever going to do. How were we going to keep the businesses going? What about all the cows? What about the fields? I knew we could get through the next few days, but then what? I had no idea where the books were. How was the business doing financially? Spring was coming, and we would need to plant corn soon. We needed to feed the cows. Calving season would start any day.

Lying there with all that grief, uncertainty, and anger, eight months pregnant, I made several decisions that got me through that night—and changed the course of the rest of my life. First, I was going to make Dad proud of me. No matter what I did, I would live my life to make him proud. Second, I was going to help keep this farm going.

Chapter 9

The Good Mess

Kassidy was born on April 21, 1994. She was a reminder to our whole family that we could be happy again. Death is an inevitable part of life. But so is new life.

This little girl was perfect in every way, and we named her Kassidy Corinne after my mother. Mom loved that. Kassidy was the first grandchild on either side of our family. She was a happy baby—just an angel. From the time she was a year old, we could tell she was eager to please. She was so loving and kind. She loved to help me with chores and if there was ever an inkling of mischief, I could give her a look and say "Kassidy, no," and she would say, "Yes, Mama."

She spent a lot of time with her grandma or with Aunt Kim when I was working. And I worked a lot of hours through the rest of that year and was so thankful for family who helped care for her. As she grew, Kassidy also spent a lot of time with me in tractors, riding in combines, or doing chores. One night during harvest when she was four years old, we were finally going to quit combining around two o'clock in the morning. Kassidy was still playing with her toys on the floor of the combine cab.

"Kassidy, pack up your toys now," I told her. "We are going to go home soon."

"Jus' a minute, Mama," she said, still playing with her Barbie on the floor of the giant cab.

"Kassidy, I said pick up your toys. We are done for the night. Let's go."

"Jus' a minute, Mama," she repeated.

I had been working all day. It was two o'clock in the morning. I was exhausted. I wanted to go home.

"Kassidy Corinne," I said more sternly. "You pick up those toys right now, do you understand me?"

She rolled her eyes and put the Barbie in her toy bag. And then she muttered under her breath, "Somebody's crabby!"

She was right! But her little comment made me laugh and reminded me of my blessings.

Our second daughter, Kennedy, was born three years later, in 1997. It now became clear that I was no longer needed, because Kassidy decided *she* was going to raise this one. Perhaps it was because she was the oldest, perhaps it was just her personality, but it seemed that over the years, Kassidy became the second mom—to her sister and brother and all her cousins too.

Since my siblings and I all worked together every day, we brought our kids to the farm with us in the morning. The whole crew of them would be together all day. And since Kassidy was the oldest, she always took charge. In fact, she became quite the little boss. None of the cousins dared step out of line with her around.

Kassidy set the agenda early, gave all of them their responsibilities, and made sure they all stayed on task whether it was work or play. When she was six years old, she came to me and asked permission to spank her sister and cousins because "they needed it."

She was a natural leader right from the beginning.

Kennedy was the sweetest baby we had ever seen. She almost never cried. She was always happy. This was odd, since she had a terrible case of reflux. As soon as she ate, she would throw it all back up—but she would smile all the while.

We put her on a special kind of formula that smelled terrible but was supposed to help. It was super expensive, and it made Bryon want to cry every time she spit any of it up. She would drink a bottle and then throw up half of it and Bryon would say, "Well, there's $5 we will never get back."

The doctors told us she would probably outgrow it by the time she was a year old. So we kept her draped in bibs or lying on huge quilts in the middle of the floor. If anyone went near her, we would warn, "Don't pick her up!"

But it never bothered her. She would just throw up. Then smile. Thankfully, the doctor was right. At almost exactly one year old, she just stopped throwing up.

Five years after Kennedy came along, we had Booker. He was a bit of a surprise. When we found out we were pregnant and that we were going to have a boy, I knew we were in trouble. For twenty years, my grandpa had wanted a grandson or great-grandson to be named after him. No one had taken him up on it, though, because Grandpa's name was Alf Harold Bergan.

Nobody could picture their sweet baby boy as an "Alf."

We loved our grandpa, who was a proud Norwegian. But we also loved our children. That would be quite a handle to put on one of them.

To keep Grandpa happy, everyone in the family kept telling him that they were saving "Alf" for Bryon and Kristi—knowing it was unlikely we were going to have any more children. Anyway, even if we did have another child, there was at least a 50 percent chance it would be a girl. So, once we found out we were expecting a boy, we knew we were in trouble.

Debating names back and forth, Bryon and I finally decided we would call our baby boy "Bergan." We hoped that Grandpa would be happy we had at least used his last name. It really was our best option.

But when our son was born and the nurse asked what we planned to name him, Bryon replied matter-of-factly, "Booker."

"Booker?" I asked, confused.

"Yeah, 'Booker,'" he said. "I like it."

"His name isn't 'Booker,'" I replied, still lying in the hospital bed where I had just given birth to the child. "It's 'Bergan.' Like we decided."

"No, I like 'Booker,'" Bryon replied. "It's a good baseball name."

Sensing some tension, the nurse left the room.

I turned to Bryon. "We have to name him 'Bergan' after Grandpa. We have to! This is not negotiable. You never even mentioned the name 'Booker' to me before."

I was steamed.

"Besides, 'Booker' is not a name! You can give it to him as a nickname, but all his friends will call him 'Booger' and he will be teased," I added.

Bryon just looked at me and said: "I like 'Booker.'"

We were at an impasse.

Two days later, Bryon arrived at the hospital to pick us up. We still had not agreed upon a name and we could not take our new baby boy home until his name was on the birth certificate.

Bryon walked into the hospital room and said, "I looked up what 'Booker' means last night. It means 'Bible lover.' How could you not want your child to be named 'Bible lover'? Isn't that what we would want for him? To love the Lord and Scripture?"

Well, he had me there.

So, we named him "Booker Alf Noem." And we got to leave the hospital.

For almost a year after Booker came home, I had a hard time telling anyone his name. But in time, we all came to realize that the name fit.

He did play baseball when he was young.

And he loves the Lord.

Grandpa cried happy tears when we told him his great-grandson's name. It was perfect.

Before he became a baseball player, Booker was a pretty sick little boy. He had a lot of breathing issues and spent quite a bit of time in and out of the hospital. He took regular breathing treatments on a daily basis and steroids and other medication to keep his lungs open so he could get enough oxygen. He didn't eat much and had a difficult time gaining weight.

When he was five years old, we could finally afford to build a new house and tear down the little farmhouse we had been living in since we got married. It needed extensive repairs beyond what was reasonable and was impossible to keep warm in the winter. When we tore the house down, we finally saw the problem causing all the issues with Booker's breathing: the walls were filled with black mold.

Within two months of moving into the new house, Booker was breathing better. Within six months, he was off his breathing treatments and steroids. He started eating, gaining weight, and his personality developed. He became such a funny, rambunctious little boy. It was like someone had given us a whole new son.

In fact, once he could actually breathe, he started to get into trouble and talked back to us. It was all pretty shocking.

I used to say to him, "Booker, stop being so naughty. Why are you being so bad?"

One day my mom heard me and bristled. She pointed her finger at me and said sternly: "Stop it! He will be whatever you say he will be. You tell him he is a good boy. That he is perfect. The words you speak over him are the words he will believe."

Feeling scolded, and realizing she had a point, I decided I was willing to try something new. So I changed the way I talked to Booker and kept telling him what a good boy he was and how wonderful he was.

Soon his behavior and attitude had changed. He rarely disobeyed or talked back anymore. It was amazing. And I learned a powerful lesson: The words we speak over people or into situations can often have a huge impact. They affect our perceptions, our self-esteem, and even our motivation to tackle everyday life or challenges. Why not approach every person and situation with an optimistic attitude and a positive declaration?

I was reminded of a sermon I heard our pastor give when I was a teenager. He gave an example of how it felt to be around negative people. He said, "Have you ever had a conversation with someone who when they walked away after the discussion you felt like they just threw up all over you?"

I remember thinking at the time that I knew exactly how that felt. I had experienced interactions with a few people over the years that made me feel discouraged and disgusted afterward. As I listened to the pastor talk about being a blessing to people, I decided I never wanted to be that person who made others feel bad after interacting with me. I didn't want to be negative, condemning, or speak poorly of others, or make them feel worse because of something I said. That sermon came rushing back to me when Mom scolded me for the way I was talking to Booker. I stopped "throwing up" on him and instead spoke words of affirmation. Everything changed.

Like most folks, we were a busy family. Maybe too busy.

I often hear people say that the secret to happiness is saying no to more things in life. That has not been my experience.

When I was pregnant with Kassidy, the ladies from our church hosted a baby shower for me at one of their homes. During the party, they went around the room and each lady offered me one piece of advice I would need as a new mom.

The women handed out the usual words of wisdom—take a nap when the baby does, get on a schedule right away, and make sure you take a break from time to time.

When it got to my grandmother, my dad's mom, who was a tough, straight-to-the point kind of woman—she offered a surprising bit of advice. I have never forgotten it.

"Kristi, say yes as much as you can—because so many times as a mom you *have* to say no."

Those words resonated with me. I didn't want to be a mom who said no to everything my children found exciting or wanted to do. I decided then and there that I was going to be a mom who said, "Yes!"

If my kids wanted to race me down the driveway, we raced down the driveway—and it was a *long* driveway. If my kids wanted to jump in a mud puddle on Easter Sunday in their church clothes, we jumped in a mud puddle. Whatever we did, we did with all our energy. We tried new things, met new people, and had new experiences—all the time.

I applied this advice to my own life as well. I decided to say yes to every opportunity I could. I would try whatever it was and if I didn't like it, I could stop and try something else. That simple piece of advice from my grandmother has made all the difference.

Not to say that it always led to the most productive or profitable results. For example, I tried quilting, but I found my compulsive tendencies a detriment to the quilting process. I have a strange inability to stop a project once it is started. After sewing and not sleeping much for four days because I couldn't relax until the quilt was done, I remember my mom patting me on the hand while I was hunched over a sewing machine one night, refusing to go to bed.

"Maybe quilting isn't for you," she said. She was right.

Same thing happened with scrapbooking my kids' pictures. Our two girls, Kassidy and Kennedy, have their childhoods displayed in beautiful books I completed in just days. They are filled with notes and dates and wonderful memories. But once I finished and had all their pictures neatly laid out in the books, I realized I wasn't enjoying the process. I had just created another thing on my to-do list that was a job rather than something fun to do.

So I decided I needed to take scrapbooking off my list. Most of Booker's pictures are just thrown into a drawer in our office. Poor Booker.

Because I always tried to say yes, I became a children's pastor and a 4-H leader. I trained horses, raised dogs, started a hunting lodge, and ran for public office. And best of all, I got to meet so many of the most amazing people in my life today—all because I learned to say yes when I first became a mother.

I believe that saying yes can change your life. That one event you agree to go to, the committee you join, or the job you try might open the door that changes your life forever. You may meet the person who becomes your next boss. Or your next business partner. Or you may find that you have an undiscovered gift or talent, or find joy in something that you'd never tried before. Say yes to new opportunities. You don't have to do them forever, but there may be one new experience that gives you the opportunity to find the purpose of your life you have always been searching for.

Chapter 10

Rookie

After Dad's passing, we continued working every day as a family on the farm. Bryon and I ran the hunting lodge. My mom had also bought a restaurant in Watertown called Past Times. She had always dreamed of owning a restaurant and she found this incredibly rewarding, if also exhausting. I helped her keep the books and manage employees. In many ways, our family was as economically productive as we had ever been. Yet I was also learning just how much the government—especially the federal government—interferes with every aspect of life as a business owner.

Our Founders never dreamed that bureaucrats in Washington, DC, would hold so much power over family farmers living and working the land fifteen hundred miles away. Today, it's basically a full-time job for farmers everywhere to keep tabs on all the various requirements and weigh in on the policies that dramatically impact your way of life. You do all you can to obey the rules while you try to scratch a living out of the dirt, hoping all the while for favorable weather and a good market. As you work, you dream of your kids and your grandkids walking across the same fields, pastures, and hills. You want to make sure that the land you've been blessed with stays valuable and productive for generations to come. So you lobby for sensible changes, but so many things feel out of your control.

At some point over those years, I realized that a lot of these changes just were not going to happen unless I decided to do something about it. Myself. I had been raised to believe that you don't just complain about things, you fix them.

What that looked like exactly wasn't all that clear to me. But I was starting to get an idea.

In 2006, a seat came open for our district in the state House of Representatives. I had previously served on the South Dakota Soybean Association board. We worked on policy at both the state and federal levels, which gave me leadership opportunities that built my confidence and further piqued my interest in government policies.

US senator Tom Daschle had also appointed me to serve on the South Dakota Farm Service Agency state committee. The committee was made up of producers who helped oversee the federal farm policies in the state, so it came as a shock to many that Daschle, the Democrat majority leader in the US Senate, would appoint me, a Republican. People wondered for years if maybe I switched to the Democrat Party to serve; of course, I never did, and to his credit Senator Daschle never asked.

I first got to know Senator Daschle shortly after my dad died, when I started showing up at farm policy meetings. Many federal policies were dramatically impacting our operation, and I needed to know more about them if we were going to make it. Senator Daschle invited me to a retreat in the Black Hills he held every year to recruit and train future leaders. There would be only about twenty people there, and I knew the goal was to get me to run for office as a Democrat.

Now, I would never be a Democrat, but I couldn't think of a good reason *not* to go. I figured the connections could be helpful in business. I was also smart enough to know that it's helpful to be on a first-name basis with anyone making major decisions on policies impacting your family. It was a weekend filled with listening to speakers, hiking, and dinners. There was still a lot of time for one-on-one conversations with Senator Daschle, and he was candid about life in a public role and some of the challenges of serving.

I didn't realize until years later how much attending that retreat would cause Republicans to doubt my conservative credentials. Even back then, any attempt at bipartisanship was seen as a weakness to partisans and the party faithful. First, that's wrong, and second, my view of it was strategic. Gathering more information on those who may be adversaries on policies or positions is always a good thing. More insight into what the opposition thinks and who they are recruiting could only help, not hurt.

Fast-forward to 2006 and that open state legislature seat. I floated the idea to my family to see if they thought it was a good idea. Honestly, it was a bit strange for us all; no one in my immediate family had considered public office before. We weren't really "into" politics. But I had volunteered to help several candidates I believed in before, and I figured we needed someone in the legislature who was still active in agriculture and business.

I remember my father-in-law, Al Noem, thought I would be great. Al is a thoughtful, quiet-spoken man who has always given me great advice. He wasn't necessarily political, but he knew the area and people. He suggested I visit with his neighbor Dean Anderson. Dean had been the secretary of agriculture in South Dakota and his daughter Deb had been the first woman Speaker of our state's House of Representatives. I didn't know Dean, but I thought the world of my father-in-law, and I needed all the insight I could get if I was going to consider putting my name on a ballot.

Running for local office is just like saying to all your friends and neighbors, "What do you *really* think of me?" And they'll be honest because you'll never know how they voted. That's truthfully quite frightening. Those in your everyday life know you the best. *What if I lose?* I remember thinking. *How would I hold up under a vote of "no confidence" from the people who know me best?* I wasn't sure I should take the risk.

I drove my pickup over to Dean's for coffee. His sweet wife, Marilyn, welcomed me to the kitchen table where Dean was reading the paper. I remember sitting in the kitchen, the smell of the coffee and the crinkle of his paper as he put it down. Dean was a perfect stranger at that point, yet there are moments when you simply get a feeling about someone. I felt instantly that I could trust him to tell me the truth. We talked awhile, and then Dean patted my hand and said, "You would be wonderful, Kristi. You should do it."

"And," he went on, "if you need any advice or want me to write a letter endorsing you, I will sure do that. We need young people like you. You remind me of my Deb."

I decided to jump in.

I had a primary and a general election to win. We worked hard, went to meetings and parades. We put up signs and knocked on doors. I ended up winning the election, and the next day I got a phone call from my brother-in-law, Wesley, a doctor up in Pierre, our state capital.

"I have a place for you to live during the session in Pierre!"

I was shocked, because I hadn't even thought that far ahead.

"Where?"

Wesley had been in surgery that day with an orthopedic surgeon and told him that I had just won a seat in the legislature the night before. Wesley asked this doctor if I could live with him and his wife during the forty-day session that would be starting in two months. Since the capital was three hours from our ranch, I would need to drive there every week for session and then come home on the weekends. Apparently, this doctor had agreed to host me, a stranger, for the forty-day session coming up.

"Wesley!" I said. "These people don't know me! I don't know them! You want me to move into their house with them?" Wesley assured me it would be fine, that Dr. Steve Stout and his wife, Peggy, were wonderful people I'd love. He was absolutely right.

When session began, it was like going to college again. Pack up some belongings, go stay in a town during the week, go to lots of meetings, meet new people, and come home on weekends. Except I still had all my work to do at home. It was extra hard, though, because I was focused on being savvy and not making any mistakes. (Not sure I had the same focus during college.)

The wheels fell off the bus within a couple of weeks.

My husband's cousin Brock Greenfield was also in the legislature, and we represented the same district. He was very involved in the pro-life movement. I am passionately pro-life and was very supportive of moving legislation during my first session that I believed was the right path forward for South Dakota.

Brock did not think it made sense strategically, and I just could not believe that we disagreed on this. After meeting with a group of legislators about it, I was frustrated that Brock had openly opposed moving the bill. I decided I was going to send an email to a few supporters back home and let them know about the discussion and ask them to contact Brock. That was not a good idea. Within a couple of hours, my email was posted on a prominent political blog with a commentary discussing how I, as a brand-new legislator with no experience, was questioning a stalwart of the pro-life movement on the best legislative strategy.

The article made me sound arrogant and naive...and, frankly, I was. It also sent the message to everyone that I couldn't be trusted. If I disagreed with someone, I would start attacking them with emails to constituents. I knew this was not who I wanted to be, and that I had made a big mistake. I also realized that not many of my fellow legislators were necessarily going to want to be friends or work with me on issues if this was my standard operating procedure.

Later that day I was sitting at my desk, trying to keep my head down and work when then majority leader Larry Rhoden suddenly appeared. Larry is a cowboy and a seasoned veteran of South Dakota state politics. Plainspoken. Tough. He had heard about my mistake. It was something he'd *never* do. I braced myself for a firm dressing-down, but to my complete surprise, Larry asked if I wanted to go to dinner with him and a small group of people that night. I immediately said yes, and we made plans to meet up at the local Chinese restaurant in a few hours.

When Larry tells this story, he says he asked others to

join us like this: "Why don't you come to dinner tonight with me and Kristi? She doesn't have a lot of friends."

When I arrived, the others were already at a table together: Speaker pro tempore of the state house, Tim Rave; Senator Jim Lintz; lobbyist Matt McCaulley; and Larry. Over egg rolls and General Tso's chicken, we got to know one other. We swapped stories of ranching and family life; they talked about the issue with Brock, assuring me it would blow over, but gently advising how to do it differently in the future. They gave me the "rundown" on the other members I would be dealing with in Pierre. They also educated me on the legislative process. Here Larry led the charge, and I could tell right away that he cared deeply about parliamentary procedure. By the time the dinner was over, I was feeling worlds better.

I did not know it then, but these men would become my best friends during my years in the state legislature—and long after. From that night on, I knew I could count on them for their deeply valuable perspectives, hard-earned from years of legislative experience. They were smart, strategic thinkers who also knew when a good quip was exactly what was needed to ease the tension in a room. They are still some of my closest advisers today.

Tim and I served in leadership together in the state house when he was Speaker and I was assistant majority leader. I learned much from him about reading the room and understanding what was possible. After twenty years in the state legislature, Jim retired, but we kept him on speed dial for the institutional memory he was always willing to share. Matt was the attorney of the group and a real pathfinder who could navigate the legislative wilderness when pretty much everybody else was hopelessly lost.

And then there was Larry. Over the years, we worked extensively on property tax reform in the state house. When he moved over to the state senate, we routinely sponsored one another's bills in our respective chambers. Opinionated and tough, Larry's definitely a rancher at heart—with all the colorful one-liners that come with it. (A few of my favorites include "You can't polish a turd," "Even steers try," and "Trust me, you're wrong." There are others, but they're not things you put in print!)

One evening, though, we discovered that Larry had a surprising soft spot. After a long day of hearings and meetings, Matt offered to run over to Zesto's for some of the best ice cream in South Dakota and pick something up for each of us. (I love ice cream, and it's an all too frequent way to end my workday.) Matt took requests from Tim and me. Then he got to Larry. Without a trace of embarrassment, Larry gave his order: "butterscotch malt." We couldn't believe it. Larry, the rough and ready rancher, wanted a *butterscotch* malt, just the sweetest, most froufrou thing on the menu. We've never let him forget it.

The four of us were also big fans of the hit NBC show *Seinfeld*. One evening, as we sat around the capitol talking about our favorite episodes, Matt suddenly had a realization: Larry, he said, was a lot like Kramer, with his funny expressions and crazy head tilts. Matt had a lot of similarities to Jerry. *I* had plenty with Elaine. Then we all turned to look at Tim, who suddenly realized he was *George*. And in classic Costanza fashion, Tim blew up in protest—arms flailing everywhere, protesting loudly. We died laughing.

Over the coming years, the four of us would end up working long hours together and spending time with one another's families. In a funny twist of fate, more than a decade after that first dinner, I would ask Larry to be my running mate as lieutenant governor. We'd come a long way from the Chinese restaurant in Pierre, but I was just as grateful when he took me up on this offer.

And no, he hasn't lost any of those crazy expressions.

While in the legislature, I was passionate about tax policy. Besides reforming how our agricultural land was taxed in the state, I also brought forward provisions on wind energy tax reforms and served on the taxation committee to fight off new taxes in the state.

Every year, there were new proposals to raise taxes on everything, and I was proud of the low tax, low regulatory environment we had in the state of South Dakota. It took constant focus to keep our state a friendly place to raise a family and run a business. As one person told me when I first was elected to the state legislature: "Kristi, just remember, every day you are in session, our way of life is in jeopardy."

Meaning that sometimes, the best thing you can do as a legislator is stop the bad bills from becoming law.

One of the best teaching moments of my legislative experience was when a cigarette tax change was being debated. It had failed in previous years and a bill had been filed again the first year I was assistant majority leader. I was working in my office when I heard a knock on the door and looked up to see Jeremiah Murphy standing there. Now, there were two Jeremiah Murphys—a senior and a junior. It was Jeremiah senior standing in my doorway.

Jeremiah Murphy senior was a wonderful human being.

"May I visit with you quickly?" he asked. Jeremiah was a longtime respected lobbyist who was very effective for his clients. He had a wonderful, warm personality and eyes that danced with humor while he convinced you his preferred plan of action on legislation was the right one. He was always kind, wise, and someone who took the time to teach less experienced legislators the importance of the institution and legislative process but did so in a way that didn't make you feel stupid or ignorant. I respected Jeremiah a lot.

I invited him into my office and he sat across from my desk.

"How are you feeling about this cigarette tax debate this session?" he asked.

I started to speak about where the bill was and how I was considering evolving my views on it. He listened quietly until I was finished. Then he pulled a little tape recorder out of his pocket and said, "Let's see what you had to say about this tax two years ago in committee." He pressed Play.

I heard my voice fill the room. I was making a passionate statement regarding my position on the bill, and Jeremiah and I listened for several minutes before he stopped the tape.

"I just thought you might like a reminder."

He stood up and quietly left my office.

I sat there thinking about the education I had just received. How words matter. That as a public office holder, my words would live forever, and if I changed position, I needed to be able to explain why. And that other people were listening to me and paying attention. They would judge me based on what I had said, even if I had said it years before. And that perhaps my best argument was the same one I had been using for years. That foundational truths don't change if they are truly important. I was so grateful for a wise man who took the time to teach a young leader this valuable lesson. We need more Jeremiahs in the world.

When I first came into the legislature, one of my good friends there was Tom Brunner. Tom represented a rural part of South Dakota and had a wonderful family that stayed with him in Pierre for the legislative session. His wife would often invite me over for dinner at night and I so enjoyed getting to know all of his children and having family discussions during the middle of the week, even though my family was hours away. They treated me as if I were part of the family.

But when I decided to run for assistant majority leader, I learned that Tom was thinking of running too. He came to me and told me he thought I needed to wait, that I hadn't been in the legislature as long as he had, and I should pull my name out of the running. I didn't feel right about that. I knew I had support and thought we both should stay in the race and accept the outcome. Tom got upset with me, but, honestly, I thought he would get over it once the leadership elections were over.

He didn't. When I was elected to the position, he shook my hand, walked out the door, and didn't talk to me again for years. In fact, over the years, he has been openly critical of me and still keeps his distance. I'm sure I could have handled the situation better, and perhaps I did things that were offensive to Tom that I am not remembering. But sometimes relationships just end. And that will always grieve me. These situations make me more aware of how important communication and forgiveness are. I miss Tom's friendship, but I also believe that sometimes relationships change and that's okay too.

I used to think that policy expertise alone was the most important part of serving in the legislative body. Making laws and repealing statutes both dramatically impact people's lives, after all. But knowing the ins and outs of policy doesn't automatically translate into effectiveness. I learned from Larry, Jim, Tim, Matt, and so many others I met in those early days in the legislature that I really am in the people business. And whenever I ask older, wiser politicians to reflect on their time served, they usually regale me with stories of personalities, interactions, and characters encountered over the years. In a word, they tell me about the *relationships* that made the policies possible.

I think this holds true no matter what field we're in. Some folks may remember our work, but most will remember how we make them feel—how we treat them, how we invest in them. This wasn't something I knew coming into Pierre. I know it now. If you want to change people's lives, you first have to care about people's lives.

Chapter 11

Nudges

February 2010: It was a raw, subzero day of slate gray skies, the kind that finds cattle hiding behind windbreaks to keep warm. I was sitting in my office in the state capitol building in Pierre, planning the day's schedule. I had served in the state legislature for four years, and while the marble corridors were a far cry from the ranch, I felt comfortable enough by now. I had established a pretty good reputation for working hard and taking up serious issues facing the people of South Dakota—at least enough that I'd been chosen by my colleagues to serve as assistant majority leader. The role brought a lot of responsibility, and being successful in the job depended on building relationships with fellow legislators and working to find common ground. I liked it.

That morning, I was staring down committee hearings in half an hour, before more meetings with Majority Leader

Bob Faehn and Speaker of the House Tim Rave to double-check the calendar for action on the house floor in the afternoon's legislative session. Like most office jobs in America, mornings were typically pretty busy. In the capitol, legislators might stop by to discuss issues they were passionate about. Lobbyists often stuck their heads in the doorway to see if they could "educate" me on whatever they were being paid to promote that particular day.

It was not long before the hearings were scheduled to begin when my phone rang. I recognized the number right away.

"Hi, Kristi, it's Suzanne!"

I'd known Suzanne for over a year now. A highly respected businesswoman from Sioux Falls, she had formed close ties to the state Republican Party as a result of her work helping John Thune beat Senate Majority Leader Tom Daschle in 2004. It had been the biggest race in the nation that year, and all eyes were on South Dakota as money and people poured into the state to take out the leader of the Democrat Party in Congress. Suzanne had been instrumental in that grassroots effort and helped lead "Women for Thune."

Suzanne was a doer.

We had met over a year earlier, along with Barb, another Sioux Falls businesswoman who had a real no-nonsense attitude and sharp political smarts to match. Suzanne and Barb had been given my name by someone (no doubt a member of Thune's team) who hinted that I might not be a bad recruit to run against South Dakota's then sitting US congress-woman, a Democrat named Stephanie Herseth Sandlin.

It was a full-court press from then on.

Stephanie was a "Blue Dog" Democrat, fairly popular in the state despite her party affiliation. She was known for being moderate but cast liberal votes when Washington Democrats needed them. A close friend with Speaker of the House Nancy Pelosi, she also had big aspirations: Stephanie was known to be eyeing a US Senate seat, more than likely as a challenger to Senator Thune in the near future. Everyone knew Stephanie would be tough to beat in a fight for a Senate seat, and the thinking went that someone had to take her on before she could pull the trigger.

It's funny how politics works: you never can be sure of people's real motivations. It was a close Thune supporter who first suggested I run to unseat Stephanie. I admit I wondered whether that person truly wanted one more Republican in the House of Representatives, or if they really just wanted Stephanie beaten at the polls statewide before she could come after John. Whatever the initial motivation, Barb and Suzanne were pressing hard.

They weren't having much luck, though.

When they first approached me, I told them I had zero interest in being a member of Congress. I was farming and ranching with my family, raising three little kids with my husband, managing the hunting lodge, helping with the family restaurant, and serving in the legislature in a leadership role. No way was I interested in getting on a plane every week and leaving everything I loved to go argue with politicians in hot and humid Washington, DC. It just was not feasible. It was nice to be asked. Thanks, but no thanks.

But here Suzanne was, calling again that chilly February morning.

"Hi, Suzanne," I replied. "How can I help you today?"

"I know you are busy in Pierre," she said, "but I wanted to ask you something. Yesterday, I was in church, and I couldn't get you off my mind. I just kept thinking about you, and when church was over and I was leaving, Barb came running up to me in the parking lot. She grabbed my arm and said, 'Suz, I don't know why, but I couldn't get Kristi off my mind today during the service! I think we need to call her again.' So, Kristi, Barb and I just wanted to check in and see if there was any way you might have changed your mind about running for Congress?"

I told Suzanne that no, I had not changed my mind. At all. In fact, the thought seemed even more impossible as it was now February, and South Dakota's primary elections were held in June, and there were already two very good candidates running on the Republican ticket. To jump into a primary this late in the game and win would be close to impossible—especially for someone like me who had almost zero name recognition in most of the state.

"Well, would you at least continue to pray about it?" Suzanne asked.

I assured her that yes, Bryon and I would continue to

pray about it. I thanked her for the call and went back to work.

Mere moments later, the phone rang again.

This time, I didn't recognize the number, but when you're assistant majority leader, you don't get to ignore calls during the legislative session. You answer and do so quickly. Time was short. There were bad bills to kill and a budget to pass.

"Could I speak to Kristi Noem, please?" The voice was unfamiliar.

"This is Kristi."

"Hi, Kristi, my name is David and you don't know me. I live in California and my son used to work for George W. Bush. We were talking the other day about the momentum that Republicans are seeing this year across the country in these congressional districts, and that we really needed to recruit a few more candidates to run and win so we can get the majority back in the House. We need a candidate in South Dakota who can beat Herseth Sandlin. Have you ever thought about running for Congress?"

I laughed. I had never met this guy before. I had no idea why a Californian would even be bothering about a congressional race in South Dakota. I politely told him people had been talking to me about it for over a year, off and on, but that my husband and I had decided that going to Washington, DC, was not something we wanted to do.

David and I chatted for a few more minutes about politics and candidates and legislation. He was very kind, and before he hung up he assured me that if I changed my mind about getting on the ballot, he would be there to help. I hung up the phone and shook my head and laughed a little about the coincidence of the two calls coming so close together.

Then my phone rang. Again.

This time it was Ed Metzger—a family friend from Georgia who had hunted on our land for several years with a group of people who had become almost family to us.

Ed got right to it: "Kristi, some friends and I were just talking last night about the upcoming elections—have you and Bryon ever considered running for Congress?"

This time there was a long pause.

After another long minute, I took a breath and answered Ed.

"Well, now I am."

Three calls in less than half an hour.

None of the three callers knew one another.

All had the same message: run for Congress.

As a person of faith, I own that there are coincidences, and then there are moments when God taps you on the shoulder. If you read the Gospels, you'll see that the Lord is a pretty persistent person who has no problem surprising people with things He'd like them to do. I'd known this all my life, but that made it no less irritating that February morning in 2010.

Truth be told, I am a pretty decisive, opinionated, and hardheaded person. I certainly don't like to think of myself as someone who has to be nudged to do anything. But as I sat at my desk in the state capitol, a place I'd come to enjoy, a place that was *familiar* to me, I began to wonder: *Is God asking me to go somewhere else? Someplace I might not be so comfortable?*

As Ed and I talked, I couldn't shake the feeling that the Lord was up to it again. And if so, it had to be because I had something to offer that nobody else had. Something unique to me.

Ed and I had a pretty lengthy discussion about the realities of such a race and what it would mean for my family. He felt that my business background and life experience—as a family rancher, a small business owner, a mother—were exactly what we needed in Congress. The whole time we were on the phone, however, I just kept thinking, *What is Bryon going to say?*

Before we hung up, I promised Ed I would talk to Bryon again and that I'd follow up with him in the next few days.

Then I called home. It was still early, and I knew Bryon would be getting the kids ready for school before he headed out to work. I could hear the familiar sounds of mornings at our home in the background. Our kids chattering. The dog barking.

With a lump in my throat, I told Bryon about the calls.

"What are you trying to say?" my husband asked.

"Listen, at this point, I am worried about us being disobedient to what God may be asking us to do," I answered. "I know this is not something we *want* to do. And I'm not saying He is for sure asking us to run. But honestly, if we lose, they'll quit bothering us. If we were to win—which seems almost impossible—well, then we would know for sure it's something God had His hand in."

On the other end of the line, Bryon was quiet. I tried to see it from his perspective. I knew he didn't like me being gone for the few weeks that the legislative session took place in Pierre. The thought of my going to DC to work every week, year-round, had to seem like a nightmare to him.

But there was more to it than that. While I'm the more impulsive one in our relationship, he's always been "the reasonable adult." I am nearly always ready to jump in with both feet; Bryon stops to ask, "How is this actually going to work?"

We agreed to take the next weekend and go to the Black Hills. Stay in a cabin with the kids. Talk it over. Pray. We'd do that before we decided anything.

I hung up the phone knowing I had just ruined his day.

I wish I could say we had a wonderful time as a family that next weekend in the Black Hills. In all honesty, it was miserable.

Bryon simply wasn't in favor of our family making the run. We spent some time with the kids sledding, playing games, and talking. But the underlying current of anxiety was always there, tugging at us under the surface. We talked about it with the kids, what it would be like for them if Mom was gone a lot. Honestly, we had no idea. And the unknown made it worse.

The kids cried.

Bryon cried.

I cried.

I took a couple of walks to think and pray. The Black Hills are a good place for both—ruggedly beautiful and stubbornly silent. Passing beneath the pines, I appreciated that silence more than ever because there seemed to be so little of it anywhere else in my life.

I was getting lots of calls from people pressuring me to get into the race. Voice mails from people irritated that I would not give them a firm answer. The days were counting down to collect enough signatures to get on the ballot. The race was going to be hard enough without us "wasting more time" talking it over. But I just did not see how I could possibly do this without the support of my husband.

At one point, I left the cabin for a bit to go into town and work as there was no internet access or cell service at the cabin. I spent a couple of hours in a local coffee shop, drinking way more coffee than I should have and shooting off emails and returning dozens of missed calls.

I was still sitting in that coffee shop when Justin Cronin walked in the door. Justin was a state legislator. We knew each other well, but he was not from that part of South Dakota, so I was surprised to see him. He looked surprised to see me too.

"Hi, Kristi," he said. "What are you doing here?"

I don't know why, but I decided to tell him. Up until this time, the whole thing had been something Bryon and I had only discussed together with the political operatives who were pressuring us.

"To be honest, Justin, I'm trying to decide if I should run for Congress," I said. "I have to decide today. And Bryon isn't excited about it. We came out here to just get a break from it all. But my phone has been ringing off the hook from people who are trying to make the decision for me."

Justin's face immediately fell, and I could see that he completely understood what a big decision I had in front of me. He looked at the floor, and then after a moment, he looked at me.

"You will make the right decision," he said. "You always do."

He shook my hand and went to order his coffee. From my table, I saw him wave as he left the shop.

It was the shortest conversation Justin Cronin and I had ever had.

Justin was the funny, smart, and outgoing type of personality that people are drawn to. He was a talker, and people loved to hear him talk. There just was no such thing as a short conversation with him. Like all legislators, he no doubt had plenty of opinions he could have offered on the many things to consider. But he didn't. He let me be.

At that moment, I knew: *I am running for Congress.*

I packed up my stuff and headed back to the cabin. I didn't know what I would say to my family, but when I got in, it was clear that Bryon had done some thinking too. To be more exact, he had done some praying. My husband sat us all down at the table. Then, slowly and calmly, he told us that our family was going to run for Congress. "It's going to be hard, but we are going to do it—together," he said. "And," he added, "it's going to be a *good* thing."

While I had been out, Bryon had taken the decision to prayer, as he so often does. He told me later that he had asked God for a clear no on the whole idea but felt afterward that God had answered along the lines of "I'm not saying no to this, so you two make a decision and move on." Bryon wasn't certain that translated into "Yes, do it!" But he was confident this would be something that God would bless if we chose it. With his characteristic humility, Bryon said yes.

With Bryon on board, the decision was made. And it would not be just me running for Congress; it would be *us*. We still didn't know completely what we were in for. The anxiety was still there. But our family left the Black Hills with a confidence we didn't have when we'd arrived.

The decision to run for Congress changed my family forever. Justin Cronin was a big part of it, and I was grateful for the quiet confidence he showed in me when so many others outside our family were just adding noise. Sadly, in November 2020, Justin passed away at only forty years of age. I don't think I ever told Justin what our short conversation meant to me that day in the coffee shop in the Black Hills, but I think he knew. And I've reflected often since then how a decision that began with a series of phone calls from political operatives and total strangers ended with a short talk with a friend and the humble, sacrificial leadership of my husband.

We all face big and important decisions in life—decisions that will dramatically affect those we love. Sometimes we get nudges; sometimes we just have to make a decision and own it. Still, I think God sends us more promptings and direction than we realize, very often in the form of friends and family, and we ought to be humble enough to recognize them when they come.

Chapter 12

Outlaw at the Rodeo

W hen I decided to run for Congress, I remember having a confidential conversation with my attorney and my campaign manager about how hard the race would be. They warned me about how vicious the attacks would get. Sitting in my lawyer's office, they asked me, "Is there anything in your past that we need to know about? Anything bad that could come out during that campaign? It will be better for us to know now and be prepared than to be surprised by it when your opponent brings it forward."

I shrugged my shoulders and said, "Nothing at all— except for a few speeding tickets."

My answer was completely honest—yet somehow became the biggest understatement of my entire political career.

To this day, both of those men will tell you their greatest

mistake in that campaign was not running a background check on me—specifically on my driving record.

Then in August 2010 we received intel from a reporter that my opponent and the state Democrat Party were going to release my driving record the next day—and it wasn't going to be good.

I was campaigning in Rapid City that day, holding town halls and meeting with potential donors when my cell phone rang. It was Josh, my campaign manager.

"I just received some information that the Democrats are going to bring out against you tomorrow that says you have a lot of speeding tickets," he said.

"I told you I had some tickets."

"They say you have nineteen speeding tickets. Several for excessive speed," he continued. "One just this last March for 94 miles per hour in a 75-mile-per-hour zone—warrants for your arrest. Is it true?"

"Warrants for my arrest? I don't think so." My stomach knotted.

"Listen, when you don't pay your tickets on time, the court issues a bench warrant. It looks like you didn't pay a couple of your speeding tickets on time or something and bench warrants were issued. Is that true?" he demanded.

He sounded angry. My heart was slowly filling with dread.

"It's possible I didn't pay *some* on time. I don't know—who pays their speeding tickets on time? I don't remember," I stammered.

"This isn't going to be good," Josh said. He hung up the phone.

And he was right.

My whole campaign from that moment on became all about my driving record.

Every year in late August, the South Dakota 4-H rodeo finals are held in Fort Pierre. Kassidy had qualified and would be competing in what's known as the ambassador contest. The competition includes horsemanship skills, speeches, and interviews, with silent judges observing contestants' conduct and behavior throughout the weekend. The winner essentially becomes the official ambassador for the sport of rodeo for the next year and it's highly competitive.

Rodeo has always been a passion of both my girls, and it was something I enjoyed doing with them every weekend during the summer months. Kassidy, Kennedy, and I would load up the horses, feed, and tack, and pack everything we needed to camp out at rodeo grounds throughout South Dakota. We'd sleep in the tack room of the horse trailer, using horse blankets for bedding. For food, we ate what we had packed in coolers. And come nighttime, we would either walk or drive to the nearest truck stop to shower after a long, hot day of rodeo. Admittedly, it wasn't a relaxing way to spend the weekend, but we loved it. We loved the horses. We loved the people.

Often, Bryon and Booker would drive several hours to

watch the girls compete, but the boys rarely stayed for the camping—this was not what Bryon called "fun family time." It was my time with the girls, though, and it made them tough.

In 2010, it just so happened that the 4-H rodeo finals fell on the same weekend as my debate with Stephanie Herseth Sandlin in the town of Mitchell, South Dakota. Negotiations on the rules and details were contentious. My team was extremely nervous about the event and put me through hours of preparation and "murder boards" to prepare me to debate Stephanie, a sitting congresswoman and graduate of Georgetown Law.

I was a farmer and rancher still taking classes during the campaign trying to finish my undergraduate degree.

While no one ever admitted it out loud, my team felt I was dramatically outmatched.

A few weeks before the debate, my campaign manager called to tell me they had scheduled prep time for me the night before and early in the morning the day of the debate. I quickly informed him that I would be unable to do that—I would be at the rodeo finals with my girls during both times. He was in disbelief. We argued back and forth, and I told him he was going to have to deal with the fact that my girls and their rodeo was my priority. I told him I'd just drive down to the debate after Kassidy finished competing that morning and get there in plenty of time to be onstage when it started.

The next week consisted of phone calls and conversations

with many different advisers who did the best they could to change my mind. But I was not backing out on my girls. Nothing in their life had been normal since the campaign had started months before, and I had been gone the majority of the time traveling across the state. I was going to at least show up and help them for the final rodeo of the season.

Eventually, my team resigned themselves to the fact that we had to figure out how to make it work. The new plan: we would rent a hotel room so I could get a better rest the night before than I would sleeping under horse blankets in the back of a trailer at the rodeo grounds. I would do debate prep before I left for the rodeo. The next day after Kassidy competed in the horsemanship contest, I would leave the girls at the rodeo with friends who would supervise them. My campaign treasurer would pick me up at the rodeo grounds and drive me to the debate, where I would arrive in plenty of time to freshen up and do last-minute prep with the team before it started.

It was all going according to plan until I got to my hotel room the night before and started to get the girls showered and ready for bed. We had several other girls competing in the rodeo staying with us, too (I have never yet met a teenage girl who would pass up the opportunity to spend the night in a hotel in favor of a campground), so the room was crowded and felt like one big happy slumber party. We ordered pizza and had just started to dig in when the phone rang.

It was my campaign manager.

"There is a hit piece coming out on you tonight on the ten o'clock news," he said. "It's about your speeding tickets, and it's designed to throw you off your game before tomorrow's debate. Don't let it. In fact, don't even watch it. It's going to be bad."

As I hung up, a preview of the news segment came on the TV in the hotel room. It looked bad. The news was starting in ten minutes, and—although I told myself I shouldn't watch it—I couldn't bring myself to turn the channel.

The attack was the top news story. Produced like an episode of *America's Most Wanted*, it was horrible. The report said things like "multiple warrants for her arrest...disregard for the law...How can she expect to make the laws when she obviously doesn't follow them?"

I was so appalled I didn't even realize the teenage girls around me in the room had fallen silent. They were all watching the story, frozen like statues, pizza in hands hovering halfway to their mouths. When the segment finally cut to commercial break, one of Kassidy's friends turned slowly from the TV to look at me. Then back to the TV. Back to me. I could practically *hear* her wondering to herself, *Am I safe here in this room with that criminal?*

Kennedy, who was twelve at the time, looked at me with tears in her eyes and said quietly, "Oh, Mama."

I shut the TV off. I told the girls everything was going to be all right, desperately hoping that was true. I began tucking them into bed, reminding them that we needed to be in the arena saddled and ready to go at 7:00 a.m. For that to happen, we'd have to leave the hotel by 5:30.

I stared at the ceiling all night. The attack ad had been so bad, I wondered if I could even vote for *myself* after watching it. What must everyone think of me? I was a Sunday school teacher, our church's children's pastor, a 4-H leader. Were all those friendships and relationships with people in my community now ruined? What had I been thinking getting involved in politics?

To put it simply, I was destroyed. I simply had no idea how I was going to get on that stage the next day with any confidence that I was the best person for the job.

After a long, restless night, I got out of bed at 4:30 and got the girls ready. We left the hotel right at 5:30 a.m. My eyes were so tired from being awake all night I couldn't get my contacts in. I would just have to wear glasses that day.

We pulled into the rodeo grounds at 5:45, and I sent a few of the girls to get the horses from their stalls. Kassidy and I went to the trailer to retrieve her saddle and get her equipment cleaned and ready. We tried to be quiet as it was very early, and many people around us were still sleeping in their trailers and campers. Only the handful of families who had contestants in the horsemanship contest were already milling about on the other side of the arena.

I started to brush Kassidy's horse, Tibbs, as she went to

open up the tack room on the horse trailer. She came back quickly and whispered urgently, "Mom, the door is locked! I can't get in."

"What do you mean you can't get in? The door doesn't lock."

"It's *locked*. I can't get in."

Muttering to myself that we didn't have time for this, I tried the door myself. Sure enough, it was locked.

That's weird, I thought. *This door doesn't lock. I've never even had a key for it!*

I gave another hard pull, but the door wouldn't budge. Kassidy's eyes started to fill with tears as she realized she needed to be saddled and in the arena in fifteen minutes and all of her tack was locked in the trailer. I looked at her and said, "Look around for a big rock. I'm going to break the window in the tack room door."

We scoured the grounds until Kassidy came running back with a rock the size of a grapefruit. I decided it was big enough to give it a try.

I stood in front of the door, held the rock above my head with both hands, and swung as hard as I could at the window.

SMASH!

In the still of the early morning, the sound was like a cannon going off. Loud enough to wake the dead and everybody around us.

But the window didn't break. It wasn't even cracked.

I hauled back with the rock and swung again. And again. And again.

Nothing. Unbelievable.

Kassidy now had tears streaming down her cheeks, certain her year of practice and hard work was disappearing before her eyes.

"Go start digging through the back ends of pickup trucks," I told her urgently. "I need a tire iron. A jack. Doesn't matter what, just as long as it's heavy and made of metal."

She ran off, and I began looking in the backs of nearby trucks, climbing into pickup beds attached to campers filled with sleeping families and feverishly hoping to find what I needed without waking anyone. I searched five pickups before I finally found a tire iron and raced back to our trailer.

Once again, I swung at the window with all my might.

It worked—too well.

The tire iron shattered the window all right and kept right on going, pulling both my hands along after it, so my arms were in the window all the way up to my elbows. When I pulled them back, I saw pieces of glass sticking out of my skin and blood everywhere—on the trailer, on the ground, and running down my arms to my knuckles so that it looked like I'd just had a drunken fistfight. I reached through the window and unjammed the lock on the door. I threw the door open, grabbed Kassidy's horse blanket and saddle, and started tacking Tibbs up while she put the bridle on him. I was still bleeding everywhere, but it didn't matter. We didn't have time to do anything about it.

Tibbs was ready to go in less than two minutes. Kassidy jumped on and loped off toward the arena, with me shouting, "Good luck!" at her fading back.

I turned around, looked at the trailer with the smashed window, held up my hands, and watched as the blood ran down them, dripping into the dirt.

Dear Lord, what had I done?

Standing there in the early morning, it dawned on me. The night before, a special news story had just run across the state, supposedly exposing the dangerous lawbreaker Kristi Noem as a menace to society. Not twelve hours later, here I was, rummaging through strangers' trucks and smashing windows out of horse trailers as families and their children slept at the rodeo grounds. To this day, I have no idea how I would have explained it had anyone seen me. *Hi, I'm Kristi Noem, and I'm running for Congress. Can I borrow a crowbar?*

After taking a deep breath, I cleaned up the mess. I returned the tire iron. Then I started picking the glass out of my hands and arms. After bandaging myself up in the bathroom, I went to watch Kassidy complete her pattern in the competition. I helped her unsaddle and got the girls ready for the rest of the day and the rodeo. I hugged them goodbye and left them with my friends just as my campaign treasurer, Teddy, pulled up to drive me the two hours to the debate.

As I climbed into his suburban, he wore a shocked look on his face. I was disheveled, with bandages on my arms. My hair was a mess. I was wearing glasses. Dirt and bloodstains on my shirt and jeans.

"Don't ask, Teddy," I said tersely as he handed me coffee and a muffin.

He put on the soothing classical music he had obviously planned to play to keep me calm on the road. He had his work cut out for him.

When we got to the hotel where I would freshen up, Bryon was waiting in the lobby with fresh clothes. As I walked into the hotel room, the whole team stood. They, too, were shocked by my appearance—and incredibly disheartened. My manager asked if I intended to wear the glasses. I told him it was the only option. He asked if I had slept. I said no. He asked what happened to my hands and arms. I told him I had to break into a trailer that morning and not to ask any more questions.

It was going to be an interesting day.

The debate started on time, and I looked much better than I felt. All in all, I held my own and even had a few good moments. Everyone agreed I had not lost any ground, which in our book was a victory, considering all that had transpired in the preceding twenty-four hours.

Luckily, no one seemed to have witnessed my escapades at the rodeo arena that morning. The only accusations I had to fend off were about my speeding tickets—which, at that point, were "old news."

Still, somewhere out there in South Dakota is a family to whom I am deeply indebted. If I never find you, please know how deeply grateful I am for the use of that tire iron.

*   *   *

Come election night, my campaign team and volunteers gathered at the Ramkota Hotel in Sioux Falls. It's customary for every campaign to hold a watch party once the polls close, and everyone hopes it will become a *victory* party by the end of the night. Most of the staff and volunteers gathered in the ballroom, but Bryon, the kids, and I retreated to one of the hotel rooms to wait for results as a family. It quickly became clear we would have to wait for several hours. Though I was favored, Stephanie was a strong candidate. She was experienced, and she had won her last two races by wide margins. I had never run for statewide office.

After months of relentless campaigning—meetings, ads, speeches, and handshakes—these last few hours were the most nerve-racking. But the campaign work was all over. There was nothing more any of us could do. We had run the race we wanted to run, and we just had to hope it was enough. Sitting on couches and beds, we were all pretty quiet watching the numbers go up and down on the local news.

It was early morning when the race was finally called for me, and despite all we had come through, it just didn't seem real. We didn't get long to sit with the news as a family either, because the people in the ballroom were waiting to see us.

Coming out of the hotel room, the first people we saw were John Thune; his wife, Kimberley; and their two daughters. With a big smile, John said to me, "Welcome to DC." His daughters went to mine, hugged them, and said, "Let us know if you need anything."

It became real in that moment.

When we entered the ballroom, I was shocked to see that the crowd I thought would number a few dozen or so people was in fact *hundreds* of South Dakotans—farmers, ranchers, laborers, small business owners, and families. They had all come to see one of their own take the stage as their next congresswoman. I pulled as many up there with me as I could—family and staffers and volunteers. I wouldn't say my thank-you speech was my most eloquent—let me tell you, at 2:00 a.m., *nobody* is eloquent—but the words were soaked through with the most heartfelt gratitude.

Eventually, the celebration ended, and our family trudged wearily but joyfully back to the room.

On the way, I found myself wondering: *What would Dad have thought?*

I didn't know for sure what was in store, but whatever happened in Washington, I knew one thing with absolute certainty: I was going to make Dad and South Dakota proud.

Chapter 13

Friend of the Farmer

$\mathbf{M}$y swearing-in was held at the US Capitol in Washington, DC, in January 2011. While I'd been to Washington a few times before, nobody else from either my side of the family or Bryon's ever had—and they weren't going to miss it. They packed up pickups and trailers, loading them with big Rubbermaid plastic tubs instead of suitcases (it's just easier), and road-tripped twenty-three hours out to the nation's capital. Our family is pretty big, and we got more than a few raised eyebrows from other guests as we took over the hotel. As my daughter Kennedy joked, "We definitely brought a little of the redneck to Washington."

I loved it.

Being a new member of Congress is a lot like showing up on campus the first week of college. You meet complete strangers from all over the country whom you'll have to work with and live around for the next couple of years. You sit through orientation meetings. You're assigned an office. Because Speaker John Boehner wanted me on his leadership team, I was busy in a lot more meetings than most other freshman members, meaning Bryon and my chief of staff had to make the final call on which of the available offices would be our home base the next two years. They chose one in the Cannon House Office Building, which was by that time more than one hundred years old. (Later, when I relocated to the Longworth building, my office *really was* home base. I lived and slept in that office while I was in DC. Whenever Bryon and the kids were in town, we blew up air mattresses and threw down quilts and basically had slumber parties as a family.)

Again, like college, you get to know your neighbors. Representative Heath Shuler, a conservative Blue Dog Democrat from North Carolina and former NFL quarterback, was right across the hall from us. My son, Booker, was eight years old at the time, and Heath would play football with him in the hallway. As you can imagine, Booker loved it. I always appreciated how good Heath was to my kids.

With Republicans in the majority, Speaker Boehner was eager to have the House of Representatives function as it should, holding hearings and scheduling votes—a *lot* of votes—on a regular basis. For the members, this meant a ton of walking to and from the House floor. Each House office

My dog Bo and me in the old cottonwood tree on the farm where I grew up. *Noem family photo taken by Steph Lakness Sauder*

My parents, Ron and Corinne Arnold. On their first date, Dad took Mom to a Lowell Lundstrom revival. They married and settled on the same land where Dad learned to farm. *Kristi Noem's family collection*

As South Dakota's Snow Queen, 1990. *Kristi Noem's family collection*

My husband Bryon and me. Just your typical 1990s engaged couple—sweaters and all. *Kristi Noem's family collection*

On May 23, 1992, Bryon Noem and I said "I do." Although we went to the same high school, we didn't start dating until Bryon went off to college at Northern State University. We honeymooned in LA—at Dodger Stadium. *Kristi Noem's family collection*

My daughter Kassidy was born shortly after my Dad died. Our first child, she was a reminder to our whole family that we could be happy again. Kennedy followed three years later. *Kristi Noem's family collection*

My boy Booker back when this cowboy was three years old. *Kristi Noem's family collection*

The Buffalo Roundup in Custer State Park in September 2021 is much the same as it would have been in Teddy Roosevelt's time, a century ago. "TR" is revered in the American West to this day. *Kendall Captures*

The dream team: Teddy Hustead and Beth Hollatz. True friends of our family, they have been with me since the beginning of my journey in politics. Beth has been like a second mother to our kids. *Kristi Noem's family collection*

Bryon and I at President Trump's inauguration in 2017. After the stunning upset victory, it felt as if hope for America had been restored—especially for rural communities. *Kristi Noem's family collection*

Sharing a laugh with Vice President Pence, Karen Pence, and my daughter Kennedy at the Naval Observatory. *Former Vice President Mike Pence's office*

President Trump came to Sioux Falls in 2018 for a rally during my campaign for governor. The energy was incredible. Spoiler alert: I won. *Briana Sanchez / Argus Leader, Sept. 7, 2018*

With outgoing Governor Dennis Daugaard and his staff during a transition meeting on the state budget. *Matt McCaulley*

The backyard of the governor's residence in Pierre overlooks the state capitol and lake. A bit different from the ranch. *Kendall Captures*

We've come a long way from high school haven't we, Bryon? *Brandon Campea Photography*

It was deeply significant to be elected South Dakota's first woman governor in November 2018 on the centennial of women's suffrage in our state. Here we are at the inauguration ball. *Bridget M Photography*

Hiking in the Badlands, where social distancing is just ridiculous. *Kristi Noem's family collection*

Transition team pheasant hunt at the farm of Paul Nelson in South Dakota. Back row: Liza Clark, Kennedy Noem, Larry Rhoden, me, Josh Shields. Front row: Herb Jones, Matt McCaulley, and Steve Westra. *Kristi Noem's family collection*

President Trump understood the needs of rural communities. He was also a firm supporter of bringing fireworks back to Mt. Rushmore. *Office of former President Trump*

My son-in-law Kyle Peters, Kennedy, me, and Kassidy in Custer State Park in 2021. *Kendall Captures*

Delivering the State of the State address in 2021. South Dakota weathered the extreme weather storms of 2019, the pandemic of 2020, and emerged as one of the nation's strongest economies in 2021. *Kristi Noem's family collection*

Hazel. She is with me all the time. *Kristi Noem's family collection*

July 4, 2020: the fireworks at Mt. Rushmore were a defiant celebration of life—the life of a nation and the lives of all continuing its story in our present time, despite the fear and pain of a global pandemic. Americans want to be free and we want to be united. *Juniper + Jade Photography*

With our granddaughter, Adeline West. I am so unbelievably grateful for this little baby and our family. I am equally determined that our country and the world will be a better place for Miss Addie to grow up. *Jordan Overturf*

Lt. Governor Larry Rhoden and I hold a town hall at the Black Hills stock show in January 2022. Larry has been a trusted friend and counselor since 2007, when he first showed a rookie state legislator the ropes in Pierre. Asking him to be my running mate was one of the best decisions I've made. *Kendall Captures*

has a little buzzer that goes off when a vote is called, and you usually get a few minutes to walk over and vote.

You get to know the people you walk with, and I became friends with Sue Myrick, another North Carolinian. Sue had been serving in Congress since 1995. She was the first woman elected to Congress from her state, and I felt comfortable asking her all the silly questions I was too embarrassed to ask others, everything from "Where's the bathroom?" to "Which way to the cafeteria?"

Most members of Congress dress extraordinarily well; Sue was especially classy. She was so elegant, and I admit I was a little self-conscious of my appearance, showing up essentially not long off the farm. Sue made me feel right at home from the start. And when she retired from Congress, she offered to let me buy some of her clothes. As a farmer's daughter, I'm no stranger to hand-me-downs and Sue's were fabulous.

The most important wardrobe decision, though, was shoes. When I first arrived in Congress in 2011, I wore heels more than I ever had at any other time in my life. With all that walking to and from the House floor, the blisters got pretty bad pretty fast. One day, as a staffer and I were on our way to the House floor, I was practically limping.

"Do you think I can wear cowboy boots out here?" I asked. "I don't see anyone wearing cowboy boots."

"Yes, you can," that staffer answered. "You're different."

I was left wondering if that was a good thing or a bad thing...

*　　*　　*

The year 2010 produced what they call in politics a "wave election." The House had flipped from Democrat to Republican hands because Americans were fed up with two years of one-party control from Democrats. Because of this, my freshman class had a lot of new, exciting faces. Some of them are still conservative champions in Congress today, like my friend Senator Tim Scott of South Carolina.

A lot of people in my class were trying to be the biggest, loudest deals to hit the Hill; I made a determined decision not to do that. This was less about keeping my powder dry and more about wanting to learn where I could make the most impact. I didn't know it then, but this would serve me and South Dakotans extremely well later, during a key legislative fight on national farm legislation. The decision to remain relatively quiet early on was a sharp move; however, I can't take credit for it.

On one of my first mornings in Washington, I had gotten up early to pray and read a daily devotional, as I'd done most of my life and still do today. This particular morning, the reading was from Matthew 10:16: "Be wise like snakes and gentle like doves" (NLV).

The devotion went on to describe how strange it is that the Scriptures would direct us to follow the wisdom of serpents. It also went into detail regarding the behavior of serpents...how the first thing they do when they come into new territory is find a place they can take shelter if necessary for protection. They find a source of nourishment and never announce their arrival when they come into a new area. They are quiet. Often you don't know they are around until you happen to stumble upon them or threaten them. But when the opportunity comes, they strike.

That's what I have to do here in Congress, I thought. *I don't have to come here and be the show and get attention. I need to observe and watch and learn who I can trust. And when opportunity comes, I need to strike.*

While most members of Congress represent districts within their respective states, some come from states so sparsely populated that they serve as the at-large representative for everyone. South Dakota is one of these less populated states, so when I got to Washington, my job was to represent *all* of South Dakota. It was a natural decision, then, to focus my time on agriculture.

Every South Dakotan—in one way or another—depends on agriculture for their living. They're either farmers, or they sell things to farmers, or they buy things from farmers. Farming is the backbone of our economy.

Control of our food supply is also a critical national security issue. We have seen wars start over oil. Imagine what could happen—how quickly the hardship would build—if another country were to suddenly shut off our food supply. Imagine grocery store shelves across America suddenly empty. At the time I write this in 2021, the supply chain shortage is already showing us how vulnerable we are and how it's in the American people's best interest to have a diverse supply chain and safe and affordable food. This is the whole reason we have farm programs.

Further, having thousands of farmers in each state—instead of just a handful—ensures more competition and lower prices for Americans. Small farmers are just as valuable as large farmers, and they deserve a level playing field. Farm programs allow them an equal chance to compete.

This is also why we need to keep our domestic food industry diversified and not allow consolidation to occur to such a degree that we lose all of our family farms and have one large corporation or interest control the production of our food. As a lifelong farmer, I have always known this in my bones. And in Washington, it has been one of those things that—for the most part—politicians in both parties have generally understood. Or, at least, they have never been hostile to the concept.

Another reason that federal farm policies are important is that there is simply no other industry that survives in such a volatile environment. I often explain it like this: Farmers will take out loans to purchase land and machinery. They may go to the bank every year and borrow hundreds of thousands of dollars under an operating note to purchase seed, fertilizer, and chemicals to plant the crop. Then they go and bury it in the dirt. They hope that the sun will shine enough, that it will rain enough, and that conditions will be favorable enough for the crop to thrive and grow and make them enough money to take care of all the payments—and hopefully have something left over.

We wait months, praying for Mother Nature to cooperate so we can go out to the field and harvest enough of a crop to get by. We may have a bumper crop one year, but find the market collapsed by elements beyond our control, like overproduction in other countries or exceptional crops in other states. We might find the price has bottomed out. Even a high-yielding crop can result in a devastating loss to the operation from market conditions we often could not predict or protect ourselves from.

You can farm for twenty years and make a good living, then have one bad year and lose everything. It is strangely a gambler's profession, and the risks bring you to your knees. And so often when I was growing up, that's how I saw my dad: on his knees, praying.

For my dad—and for so many other parents just like him, all across the country—I was going to be an advocate for farmers in Washington.

Serving on the House Committees on Natural Resources as well as Agriculture, I was heavily involved in farm bills. I sponsored several portions of them to build on the Conservation Reserve Program, a habitat program that protects wildlife and soil quality—both crucial to the long-term health of the land and the farmers whose lives depend upon it.

Historically, Washington has passed farm bills in a highly bipartisan way. Rural Republicans supported them for conservation programs that helped sustain and diversify the land

and for safety net programs for farmers. They also contained food programs that help those most vulnerable. Urban Democrats supported farm bills for those same food programs, like the school nutrition program and food stamps.

But by the time I got to Congress, things had gotten a whole lot more contentious; the farm bill had become a lightning rod in the Agriculture Committee, and this was not entirely the fault of Democrats.

After President Obama's election gave rise to the Tea Party movement, any and all spending in Washington came under harsh scrutiny. That was certainly a good thing, but it meant that even sensible spending programs—like the farm bill—fell into the crosshairs of budget-cutters. I agreed with their fiscal restraint and looked to cut any waste we could find.

But the farm bill wasn't waste. If politicians in Washington really wanted to stop wasting so much money, the farm bill just wasn't the place to start. How about foreign aid to countries that don't like us? How about all those federally funded university studies of shrimp jogging on treadmills? (look this up on YouTube; I'm not making it up.)

But Washington was Washington; even though Republicans controlled the chamber, the farm bill was languishing. For those of us from farm country, the situation was maddening.

After spending the month of August 2012 in South Dakota hearing from farmers upset at the lack of progress, I returned to Washington and immediately signed on to a discharge petition, hoping to force the farm bill to the floor for a vote—over the objection of Republican leadership. Almost a year later, in June 2013, the House *finally* put the farm bill up for a vote.

It failed.

Florida representative Steve Southerland pushed an amendment that added work requirements to the food stamps program. That idea is a worthy debate to have, but the amendment was utterly toxic—what they call in Washington a "poison pill." Attached to the overall farm bill, the amendment essentially ensured that Democrats would abandon the final bill, sealing its fate. And Republican leaders knew this.

Don't get me wrong: I am all in favor of adding reasonable work requirements to welfare. But holding hardworking farmers hostage is unfair and devastating, and a real threat to our national security. But that's exactly what Republicans in Congress did, and they knew what they were doing when they did it.

Virginia Republican Eric Cantor was House majority leader at the time. At the height of the farm bill debate, Cantor went to the House floor to argue on behalf of the "poison pill" food stamp work requirement.

I was furious.

I mean, if you care so much about requiring people to work for food stamps, fine. Pass that law. But don't destroy an essential bill in the process. Don't hold farmers hostage because you can't get your job done in Washington. And don't go imperiling American national security all because you want to make some glamorous statement on national television.

In South Dakota, our farmers were getting worried. They recognized how dangerous it was for the country to continue under expired provisions of the last farm bill. And I had been getting my head kicked in for months by Democrats back home who blamed Republicans for abandoning family farmers. They accused us of being unable to govern on historically bipartisan issues. And they had a point.

On the basic political level, I never understood how a guy like Cantor could forget that Republican members in rural districts like South Dakota needed to pass a farm bill so they could get elected—and reelect *him* to leadership. Nevertheless, Cantor's statement that day on the House floor effectively killed the bill. Republican leadership then sent their members home with no bill and no plan. Someone had to do something.

As I went wheels up for South Dakota, I remembered again the words from Matthew that I had read back on one of my first mornings in Washington: "Be wise like snakes and gentle like doves." I had lived by that every day since.

Now, it was time to strike.

The following week, at the House GOP Conference meeting, Leader Cantor got up to discuss the floor agenda. He never so much as mentioned the farm bill. When it was time for open discussion, I made my way to the microphone.

"I'd like to ask Leader Cantor to come back to the microphone," I said.

Surprised, Speaker Boehner nodded and sat down. Cantor reluctantly rose from his chair and went back to the podium.

"Could you tell me the plan for the farm bill?" I asked. Politely. Firmly.

Cantor gave a quick summary of what had happened on the House floor, conveniently leaving out the fact that he had spoken in support of the toxic amendment that led to the bill's failing. He said we would have to keep talking and find a path forward. It was the same thing I had been listening to for over a year. It was inexcusable.

The more he talked, the angrier I got. When he finished, I decided to speak frankly.

"Leader Cantor, this is unacceptable for you not to have a plan of action."

I could feel the sudden electricity in the room, but I went on anyway. I told him that, as majority leader, he controlled what happened on the House floor. This then was a question of Cantor's leadership. I told him the failure of this bill was indicative of his lack of care for his members and the constituents they represented. I also put the rest of my Republican colleagues on notice: they should expect no support from me for legislation important to their districts if they didn't care enough to understand how food got on the shelves in their corner grocery.

When I was finished, I went back to my seat and sat down.

Cantor quickly ended the meeting.

Walking into my office a few minutes later, I found my chief of staff, Jordan Stoick, pacing back and forth by the front reception desk, his arms crossed.

"What did you do?" he asked.

He'd just gotten a phone call: we were both to report to the majority leader's office. Immediately.

"I guess we'll find out," I told him. Only when we got to Cantor's office, Jordan was told to stay outside. This meeting, we learned, was going to be Cantor and Noem only. That was unusual.

Unlike most members of Congress, the majority leader gets a special suite in the US Capitol Building itself. Decorated with oil paintings and statues, it's impressive—and austere. The second I walked in, Cantor started yelling.

"You do not do that to me! You don't talk to me like that in front of the whole conference!"

Finally, he's listening, I remember thinking to myself.

As Leader Cantor read me the riot act, I politely stood my ground.

"It's past time for the farm bill to get done," I told him. "I have no intention of letting you or anyone else in Republican leadership off the hook. This needs to be a priority. I'm not going to wait anymore."

Our meeting wasn't long. But as Jordan and I left Cantor's plush suite and began the long walk back to my office, I got the feeling it had been a good one.

In the end, I and other members from agriculture states got the farm bill across the finish line and signed into law. It was a hard fight that made national news, but I think Cantor came to respect me by the time all was said and done. I'd fought for what I believed and for the people I represented—the families who grow our food.

It's a tough lesson for so many, but especially, I think, for young people today to understand. Most of us want to be liked—especially by those who are senior to us in whatever organization we belong to at the time. It's natural—part of our instinct to survive. But counterintuitively, challenging senior leaders lets them know you matter, and that they need to pay attention to you. Don't do it all the time, but do it when you need to—when it counts for people who depend on you. Those higher-ups will come to respect you for it, and that respect will go a long way.

As one example, later that summer, my colleague Representative Frank Lucas of Oklahoma agreed to fly to South Dakota to meet with my agriculture producers on my behalf. Frank was serving as chairman of the Agriculture Committee at the time, and he wanted to come personally to tell South Dakotans how instrumental I had been in getting the final bill passed.

Jordan picked Frank up at the Sioux Falls airport and drove him to the event. Along the way, Jordan asked if the chairman was traveling to a lot of members' districts to help with their reelection campaigns.

"No," Chairman Lucas answered. South Dakota would be his only trip.

"I'm doing this for Kristi," Frank said. "If a member of my committee is willing to take the balls off the majority leader to get the farm bill passed, I'm going to come out for her."

Chapter 14

Battling Bureaucrats— and Beetles

W hy do we have to work so hard *all the time*?" My siblings and I asked this question a lot growing up on the farm. Mom always gave us the same answer: "We want this place big enough that all four of you kids can stay, if you want to."

My parents' push to always do more, then, was really about preserving a possibility—a dream—that our family could stay together in the place we loved.

Of course, "doing more" did not mean you could do a lower-quality job on the day-to-day work you already had. Tractors, for example, always had to be clean. We kids were expected to maintain all the equipment and tools. My dad even preferred everyone's work clothes free from stains and holes. "No one is going to respect you until you look like you respect yourself," he would say.

For my parents, every little thing mattered.

But big things mattered too. And as I grew up, I learned that some of the biggest federal regulations mattered so much that they could actually end everything our family spent much of our time and energy working toward. In a very real sense, one stroke of a pen from a bureaucrat a thousand miles away could end our way of life.

As South Dakota's only representative in Congress, a big part of my job was making sure that didn't happen—and fighting it with every ounce of my being when it did.

One of Washington's worst assumptions is this belief that bureaucrats in a handful of federal agencies in DC know more and *care more* about the natural environment than the people who own, cultivate, and depend on that land for their very survival. In reality, there are no greater environmentalists than farmers. They *love* their land. For so many of them, it's their legacy—what they hope to leave to their children someday.

People tend to take pretty good care of their legacies.

Farmers do so because we literally live the lessons of the land in our daily work. We teach our kids how to protect it, because we'll go broke and starve if we don't. Growing up, my parents taught us how to prevent erosion and manage grazing practices to protect native grasses. We knew to plant flax strips in the fields during the fall to catch snow throughout the winter to provide more moisture in the spring. Everything we did was to protect our land.

We can debate all day long whether federal regulations help or hurt the land. We can also debate the consequences (unintended or not) of those regulations for the people who care for that land. The one thing *nobody* disputes is that every single clause in those rules, many written by the Environmental Protection Agency (EPA), takes authority *away* from citizens and families and gives it to government bureaucrats. These bureaucrats have zero connection to the land they wish to control. And in the vast majority of cases, their regulations come with massive fines, penalties, and new taxes for the real stewards of the land who earn their living from it.

In Congress, I made it a primary goal to combat the overbearing regulations aimed at putting the government in control of rural America. During the Obama administration, there was a lot to fight.

For example, in 2011, bureaucrats inside the EPA invented strict new air quality standards aimed at "fugitive dust emissions." (This would be the same dust you see in your truck's rearview mirror as you drive down a gravel road, or behind a tractor baling hay or harvesting wheat.) What it amounted to was government bureaucrats trying to penalize citizens for doing their daily work to grow America's food. Thankfully, Republicans took control of Congress. I was more than happy to be part of the effort to put a stop to that nonsense.

To my great frustration, more nonsense was soon to follow.

In 2013, the Obama administration put forward a new proposal under the Clean Air Act called the Waters of the United States, or the "WOTUS" regulation. This new requirement said that any water that could eventually end up in a "navigable waterway" was subject to regulation by the EPA and the federal government. Shockingly, this meant a drop of rain that fell in someone's driveway and then trickled into a storm gutter, drainage ditch, or stream would be under the direct jurisdiction of the federal government because that same drop could, potentially, someday end up in a major river, waterway, or the ocean.

Under this new regulation, you'd need a permit from the EPA before you could change the storm gutters on your property. The federal government would have to approve any changes you wanted to make to a drainage ditch or any similar basic maintenance. Permits under these regulations would cost thousands of dollars—payable to the federal government. And if a person was found in violation, fines of up to $20,000 per day could be levied.

If all this sounds crazy to you, that's because it is. There's no way giving this amount of control to the government could help "protect the land." What you need to understand is these regulations aren't about protecting the land. These proposals have very little to do with the environment or clean air or clean water. They have everything to do with control, power, and money.

One of the best things President Trump did was to put a stop to these proposals. His decision was a sensible, practical accomplishment that got very little attention at the time. Unfortunately, now that President Biden is in office, his bureaucrats have put these regulations right back on the table, again under the guise of "caring about the environment."

In doing so, they're choosing to ignore the hundreds of years of good stewardship by responsible landowners in places like South Dakota that show the people know how to manage the land better than the government.

To protect the land, I believe it's better to incentivize than punish. As governor, I later started the first-ever state program to encourage farmers to set aside marginal land for conservation. This is typically lowland around waterways. It's high-salinity soil, and you can't grow good crops on it anyway. Farmers would get a cash rent payment for every acre they put into the program for a period, which allows time for the soil to get into better shape, for better grasses and vegetation to grow and entice the animals to come back. It's a program that actually makes conservation financially feasible.

It's honestly not rocket science—but it *is* something that only people with a relationship and a strong interest in the land would think to try. Like a farmer.

*　　*　　*

If you have ever set foot in the Black Hills of South Dakota, you know the beauty of their silent forests. Walking among the blue spruce and ponderosa pines, you smell their sharp scent in the clean mountain air. In the fall, their pine needles sprinkle the rocky slopes, softening sounds. This, along with the stillness between the trunks and the surrounding dark, jagged peaks, can make the experience almost eerie, and always breathtakingly beautiful.

The forests are deeply important to South Dakotans. Of course, millions of tourists visit each year to enjoy Mount Rushmore, Crazy Horse, and the great outdoors. But beyond recreation and tourism, the trees ensure clean drinking water and erosion control; they also provide good jobs as the Black Hills forests are some of the few remaining that still support an operating timber industry.

But by the time I got to Congress in 2010, the forests of the Black Hills were under assault by a pernicious enemy: the pine beetle, a tiny native bug that burrows into the trees and kills them. The pine beetle is usually kept in check by hard winter freezes that kill the bugs and their larvae. However, years of warmer winters and the overgrowth of forests allowed these beetles to thrive and infest and kill more and more acres of trees.

The stands of dead timber then became fuel for forest fires. Now, the Black Hills region is home to nearly a quarter of a million people, in towns and communities scattered throughout the beautiful landscape. Good forest management was vital to protecting them and this critical wildlife habitat. The best way to control the beetles and the damage they did was through managed timber harvesting to thin the trees.

The US Forest Service has not always agreed. As a result, these stands of deadwood remained and the beetles' spread was growing out of control. This was just another example of the local community having a deep understanding of how to take care of the land, and a more distant federal government not fully understanding the picture.

The situation wasn't getting much attention from elected officials in 2010. People knew it was a growing issue, but it wasn't something that dominated conversation in South Dakota outside the Black Hills, and certainly not in Washington, DC.

I talked about the pine beetle everywhere I went.

At first, I got a lot of raised eyebrows and odd looks. At a chamber of commerce meeting in Sioux Falls, at the other end of the state from the Black Hills and hundreds of miles away from the problem, I got plenty of both from the business owners in the audience who were more interested in tax issues. That's fine and important, but I needed people to understand why they should care about those beetles in the Black Hills—and how they could help.

It was of course a different story in the Black Hills, where residents and landowners were already on board to work something out. Local lumber and timber industry leaders, business owners, and community officials were volunteering to educate others and even finance projects to get the infestation under control. But they hadn't yet achieved critical mass.

I knew there were other members of Congress with timber in their districts, members whose constituents also had disagreements with the Forest Service. So I went to work on breaking through the logjam within the US Department of Agriculture (USDA) to change forest management practices. After hundreds of hours of work, we passed a pilot project in the farm bill that covered the Black Hills, streamlining federal EPA regulations and using what's known as "Good Neighbor Authority" to cut through environmental red tape that kept us from quickly thinning stands of infected trees.

Good Neighbor Authority allows the USDA and the Forest Service to partner with states on management practices to keep forests healthy and productive. The state of South Dakota, local counties, and communities spent their own money to help log areas that previously could not be accessed because of government paperwork. We sprayed "legacy" trees to save them. We educated landowners on the danger of standing dead timber and asked them to thin their existing land to stop the spread of the horrible beetles.

It worked. Our elbow grease and creativity paid off in a partnership that eventually slowed the spread of the beetle and brought it back under control throughout most of the affected area. While there are still too many government restrictions and regulations that slow down our ability to truly manage every acre properly, today the Black Hills are as beautiful as ever.

Throughout our battle with the bugs, I kept a little jar containing a pine beetle on my desk. Every day, it served as a reminder that people's lives and livelihoods were being threatened, and that I had a responsibility to do something about it. It was also another reminder that the littlest things—if neglected—can become devastatingly destructive.

In addition to its forests, the Black Hills are also home to some of America's most exquisite streams, rivers, and lakes, and people travel from across the country to try to outwit the trout that navigate these pristine waterways. In the city of Spearfish, the D.C. Booth Historic National Fish Hatchery and Archives is one of the oldest hatcheries in the country. Established in 1896, the hatchery is a nonprofit dedicated to maintaining trout populations in the Black Hills, and the company's work has been essential to keeping our fishing tourism.

In 2013, the US Fish and Wildlife Service, in its infinite wisdom, announced plans to close the hatchery and relocate the contents of its archives to other states. This would have been devastating to the city of Spearfish and the entire Black Hills. Not only does the hatchery support the local economy with its hundreds of thousands of annual visitors, it also plays a critical role in stabilizing South Dakota's trout populations: every year, thirty to forty thousand trout are spawned and then released into waters in the region.

I was determined to not let the hatchery close.

Partnering with the local community and the Booth Society, we organized a letter-writing campaign to call attention to the planned closure. The resulting public outcry drew a lot of publicity about the threat to this unique piece of American history. Meanwhile, back in Washington, I began educating my colleagues in Congress—especially members of the Appropriations Committee—about the hatchery's importance.

"Look, this is a shining example of the American West," I'd tell them in conversations on the House floor. "We've worked to keep it thriving, but if we lose this, there's really nothing to replace it in the entire country."

I'm sure it helped that a good many of my colleagues, Republican and Democrat, love fly fishing themselves. This makes a lot of sense: as a member of Congress, so much of your time is not your own, and there's nothing quite like fishing to restore some inner calm. I could practically see the wheels turning in their heads as I asked them to imagine *not* being able to get away for a fishing trip.

This wasn't my first rodeo.

It took over a year, but in the end, the US Fish and Wildlife Service announced that not only would they keep the hatchery open, but they would also make it the National Archives for the *entire* US Fish and Wildlife department, essentially securing the future of the hatchery for quite a long time to come.

It was an important win, and I offer it here to make

the point: no one understands our outdoor heritage better than the people closest to it. It's also a foundational part of being conservative. Conservatives, after all, *conserve*. When it comes to the land, this is what real environmentalism is all about.

Chapter 15

Beating the Beltway Mentality

There is something profoundly humbling about serving in Congress. If you read our nation's history, you understand that you're continuing an experiment in human freedom that began hundreds of years ago and that has continued, however imperfectly, ever since. The most fundamental concept behind it all is that the politicians have no power on their own. All of it comes from those they represent. Sometimes the people can surprise you with what they decide. But no matter who you are, no one is above the people.

June 10, 2014, was primary election day in Virginia, and Congress was in session in Washington, DC.

Every member of the House knew Eric Cantor, the Republican majority leader, had a primary challenger that year. Eric was expected to dispose of Dave Brat fairly easily; and in the days leading up to the election, he didn't appear too worried about losing. As Eric left town that day to head to his home district for his victory party, he assured us all he would be back the next day to continue our work on the floor. Everyone was in for a big surprise—especially Eric.

That night, as the polls closed and the returns started coming in, it became clear that Cantor's race was tighter than anyone expected. In my office on Capitol Hill, I was glued to the television as it began to dawn on me that Cantor might actually lose. When the race was finally called, Brat was declared the winner. The political world was stunned in disbelief.

I sat in my office, wondering what this would mean for the caucus, when my phone began buzzing. It was a message from a fellow member of the House, a Republican.

"Kristi, with Eric's loss tonight, I've decided I'm running for majority leader. I'd love to have your support."

I was flabbergasted. Politically, Cantor may have been dead, but he wasn't even cold yet.

To my total surprise, mere moments later, the phone buzzed with a new message, this one from a different House Republican colleague: "I'm running for majority leader, Kristi. Will you help me whip votes?"

Another text: "Shocked by Eric's loss tonight, but we need new leadership and a fresh vision. Kristi, I need your help to run and win a race for majority leader. Can I count on you?"

Cantor had barely conceded and already people were moving on and planning *their* political future. It was pure Washington.

All in all, a dozen different members of the House blew up my phone asking for help that evening. They all wanted to capitalize on this unique opportunity that had so suddenly been thrust upon them. When I finally turned in for the night, I shut my door and shook my head in disbelief. The naked ambition I was witnessing was just disgusting. There was also a weird consistency to all the text messages, and *that* bothered me. I couldn't put my finger on just what about it felt so off.

But by the following morning, I had figured out what made me feel so unsettled by the messages. On the House floor during a vote series, I stood around discussing Eric's loss with several of my colleagues. I shared the dozens of texts I had received the night before. Then I shared my analysis of why they all made me feel so off: every single one of those texts had come from a man.

Not one woman texted me that she was interested in trying to move up the leadership ladder.

"Here's what I believe is the difference between men and women," I told our little group huddled on the floor. "When Eric lost his primary, every man in the House thought, *I would be the best majority leader ever!* And every woman probably thought, *I don't know if I have the skills to do that job.*"

There were a few laughs. Many nodded in agreement.

There have been legions of books written on the differences between the sexes. There is no end to the amount of debate and analysis one can give to the topic. Here is my simplified summary: men tend to be blessed with this wonderful confidence that allows them to look at every challenge as one more thing to take on and accomplish, while women spend more time in self-reflection and analysis, which leaves them more hesitant to jump into new situations with both feet. This isn't always true, and I'm sure you are already thinking of examples to prove me wrong. But I believe the discussion has merit, and there's a general trend of evidence to my point.

This may be why we see fewer women in leadership roles or political arenas. They may feel as though there are other people just as qualified as they are to step up and serve. More often than not, women need to be asked or encouraged to take on these types of jobs.

They don't necessarily think they need to be the ones in charge to get things done, and they don't really care who gets the credit, just as long as it *gets done*. At least that is my experience, played out in full color through a leadership election.

And as a side note, it never occurred to me to be interested in running—and no one encouraged me to either.

Perhaps that proves my point.

When I was first elected to Congress, Bryon and I made some rules for our family. First, whenever I was at home in South Dakota, our family would prioritize being together.

The kids wouldn't be going to parties or doing sleepovers at friends' houses when I was back, for example. To compensate, whenever I had any travel within South Dakota, we decided the kids could bring as many friends as they wanted along with us. I'd routinely show up to chamber of commerce meetings with a pickup full of kids in tow, only a few of which were mine.

Second, when I was in DC, I didn't want to be hanging out at Capitol Hill bars or any of the city's "elite" clubs late into the evenings while my family was more than a thousand miles away. I don't care who you are, it's just never a good idea. The only downside of this was me missing out on developing the relationships and networking with other members of Congress that I knew were so critical to accomplishing anything in a legislature.

I kept hearing about the congressional gym, though, and when I was invited by Congressman Markwayne Mullin of Oklahoma to join the morning workout crew, I decided to go. The bipartisan group met at about 6:30 in the morning—and let me tell you, they were *serious* about working out. Mullin was a former professional mixed martial arts fighter, so you can imagine what he was like at the gym. Paul Ryan's P90X routine was national news in the 2012 presidential cycle and deservedly so. I also got to know my Democrat colleagues, like Kyrsten Sinema of Arizona and Tulsi Gabbard of Hawaii, both extraordinarily hardworking members. Democrat Tim Walz of Minnesota and I had a good working relationship in Congress. Like me, he also would go home to become governor, but we've taken different approaches to the pandemic and the relationship's not quite the same. All in all, the gym was a great and healthy way to grow my network and get past a lot of the partisan grandstanding that so often happens when the cameras are on.

With Tulsi, I decided to join the congressional charity softball team to do more of the same kind of networking and outreach. Though I had never played softball before in my life, in my second year, they made me pitcher. *That* was stressful. Thousands of people come to those games. Through softball, I got to know Florida's Debbie Wasserman Schultz—always very kind to me—and New Mexico's Michelle Lujan Grisham—another one of us now serving as governor. Michelle used to bring a cooler full of Jell-O shots to the dugout. It was very competitive, and people took it very seriously.

Softball could also be pretty intense. I remember taking batting practice with Kirsten Gillibrand, now a junior senator from New York. The team would typically meet up at around 6:30 a.m. One morning, after she struck out, Kirsten took her bat and whipped it against the backstop, letting loose with a string of profanity that would make a cowhand blush. *Who talks like this at six in the morning?* I remember thinking. New Yorkers, I guess.

Serving on the House Armed Services Committee was especially significant to me. The committee is primarily responsible for funding and oversight of the Department of Defense, but its members also travel internationally with other US government officials to strengthen relationships with America's allies and partners around the world. These codelegations, or "codels" in Capitol Hill–speak, are a way to obtain firsthand understanding of the personalities, forces, and regions affecting American national security.

I was invited to travel a fair bit by House Republican leaders during my time in Congress—probably the only way this South Dakota farm girl would ever take a C-130 into Afghanistan; walk the demilitarized zone of the Korean Peninsula; fly into Scandinavia; and the dozens of other places around the world I visited with the Speaker of the House, senior defense officers, and other members of Congress. On these trips, I met and developed friendships with foreign leaders (no one impressed me more than Israel's former prime minister Benjamin Netanyahu; that guy was tough as nails) and saw up close the role the US military plays not only in our national security, but in the stability of the world.

To be clear: these trips weren't luxury vacations—just the opposite. Traveling first with Eric Cantor, then with Paul Ryan and Kevin McCarthy, they were grueling days, jam-packed with back-to-back meetings with dignitaries, military leaders, political leaders, spiritual leaders—you name it. Wherever we went, the day began around 6:00 a.m. local time and ran clear through until ten o'clock in the evening and often later.

I recall one trip to the Middle East, shortly after Paul Ryan became Speaker, that was especially busy. We stopped in Israel for meetings with Netanyahu, then traveled on to Jordan and Egypt. In between, we sandwiched in a daylong visit to Saudi Arabia. For all its history, geopolitical significance, and vistas of endless desert, my enduring memory of the place is that I was not allowed to use public restrooms because I was a woman.

Noted.

Another time, I joined Representative Tammy Duckworth of Illinois and several others on a codel to Afghanistan. We flew overnight in a C-130 Hercules—me strapped into a bucket seat alongside the humming hull of the aircraft; Tammy in her wheelchair, which was firmly secured to the aircraft's floor.

A former combat pilot in Iraq, Tammy lost both legs when her Black Hawk helicopter was shot down in 2004. Traveling inside the cold, noisy hold of a C-130 was old hat to her. It was brand-new to me. Finding it impossible to get any sleep, I finally unstrapped and slept on the floor, borrowing the lining of a Marine poncho for a blanket. Later, an officer told me my ability to fall asleep on the floor while the aircraft was knocking around had left a favorable impression on the crew. I was glad to hear it, but to be honest, I was just dog-tired.

When we landed in Herat, about fifty miles from the Iranian border, our pilots executed a tactical landing, making this massive aircraft corkscrew its way down to the landing field in case any rockets came up at us.

I was glad not to have eaten anything recently.

We were the first delegation into the city in quite some time, and the embassy where we stayed was locked down like a fortress. The next morning, I got up early to run on the facility's only treadmill. Through the window I could look down onto two reinforced concrete walls and coils of barbed wire... and a group of kids playing soccer.

This is their life every day, I thought. *They're growing up in a war zone.*

We traveled to other parts of Afghanistan to meet with our troops and leadership who were engaged in operations and partnering with security forces from many countries; we also discussed the progress of training the Afghanistan military. One evening we were to sleep at a secure facility that was running operations out of that area supporting our military engagement in the region. Black Hawk helicopters landed and took off all night long as we tried to sleep in our "hooches"—shipping containers converted into sleeping berths. The next morning, I ran into Tammy. I was exhausted from a night of no sleep because of the chaos going on right on the other side of the steel wall of my quarters.

"How'd you sleep?" I asked the combat veteran.

"I haven't slept that well in ages," she answered. "It felt and sounded like home."

Tammy Duckworth was tough as nails too.

*   *   *

Another time, Kevin McCarthy asked me to join a delegation that made a quick stop at an air base in Norway that was located close to the Russian border. This base was charged with helping the United States stay proactive by watching for any aggressive Russian activity in the region. We had strong allies in the Norwegians.

"Did you know I'm half Norwegian?" I asked Kevin. "It'll be like going home."

Somehow that fact made it back to the Norwegians—and our aircraft received an honor escort of F-16s upon our arrival. It was a touching tribute, but later we watched those same pilots demonstrate their true purpose: scrambling to get airborne in the event of a crisis with Russia. The speed and the discipline of the pilots were just astounding to see—and a sobering reminder that not everyone's geopolitical neighborhood is as safe as North America's.

But of all the trips, my visit to the demilitarized zone between North and South Korea stands out the most. When the fighting ceased in 1953—no treaty was ever signed ending the Korean War officially—the thirty-eighth parallel became the dividing line between the UN forces in the South and the communists to the north. It is the most heavily fortified border in the world, and American troops are there to this day, keeping the peace.

When I visited the DMZ, I was shocked at how close the troops on either side are to one another. Then I saw how the North Korean soldiers were trying to spit on the American forces, attempting to humiliate them in front of the news cameras. And the Americans simply took it. Stoic. Unmoving. As infuriating as it was, I could not help but marvel at how our troops maintained flawless discipline in the face of the provocation.

They were doing the hard job: keeping a war from breaking out. If I ever needed a perfect example of what America's role is in the world, it was demonstrated that day by our soldiers who stood between the two nations *literally* and kept peace.

I have a confession: I've never particularly enjoyed State of the Union speeches. Most of the time, they feel like a dog and pony show. The speeches are highly orchestrated and hyperpartisan. There's lots of standing, clapping, and fake smiling. In the hours before President Obama delivered his State of the Union speech in 2013, I was thinking about how wonderful it would be to relax in my office and watch it on TV like the rest of America. But, like most members of Congress, I headed to the House floor to hear what the president had to say in person.

The hallways were mostly deserted; other members had rushed to the floor hours earlier to get great seats where they could shake the president's hand as he passed by or appear in the television cameras' pans of the audience throughout the event.

I stood in the back. I wanted to make a quick exit as soon as it ended.

As President Obama's speech wore on, my disappointment grew. It was exactly what I'd expected: gun control, greater spending, more regulation, climate change. I couldn't help but think how it stood in stark contrast to the speech he'd given the previous year—before his reelection—when he'd spoken of tax reform, infrastructure, fighting terrorism, and supporting our domestic energy supply, including oil and gas. Now, with the election behind him, the real agenda of the Obama presidency was plain to see—and it was sprinting to the left.

Folding my arms, I began to pace along the back wall of the House floor. On several issues, I knew for a fact the president was deliberately misrepresenting the facts. In a word, he was lying. And that made me angry.

I hope he screws up, I thought. *I hope he trips over his words. I hope his teleprompter suddenly quits on him.*

God, I prayed, *let him fail.*

Immediately, I felt conflicted in my spirit: I had just made a mistake. If I believed President Obama was so wrong about so many things—and I did and I still do—then he needed me to pray for him. For conversion. For a change of heart. Not for embarrassment.

First Timothy 2:2 was a Scripture verse I had heard many times over the years, but clearly I needed to keep hearing it. It goes like this: "Pray this way for kings and all who are in authority so that we can live peaceful and quiet lives marked by godliness and dignity" (NLT).

Feeling ashamed, I realized I had come into the evening with a poor attitude and low expectations. In wishing failure and embarrassment on Obama, rather than a change in heart, I had been disobedient to what God called me to do as a Christian. And I knew better.

So there in the back of the House floor, I switched gears. I prayed for forgiveness, and then I prayed for our misguided president. While President Obama's speech certainly did not improve, the heaviness in my spirit lifted. I ended the evening more optimistic and hopeful about the coming year. The circumstances had not changed, but my heart had. And that made all the difference.

One of my deepest impressions from my time in Washington is a troubling certainty that our country has forgotten how to listen. Instead, we share our opinions louder and louder to drown others out. I believe this will destroy us if we don't change our ways. This is not to say that every opinion is equally valid. Some clearly aren't. It *is* to say that the process of weighing, challenging, and assessing all opinions has got to get better.

Right now, it's a shouting match. And I really believe it's the result of the way we have spoken to one another for a decade or more. Many—especially in the media—claim it all changed with Donald Trump. I don't believe that. And I don't think any honest observer can hold that conclusion. If anything, Trump was more of a product than a cause.

If you doubt me, go back and watch speeches from the House floor, or news interviews, or movies and entertainment from the time period beginning in roughly 2006 to where we are now. See how we have lost the art of debate. Somewhere, we as a society sadly decided it was better to destroy someone's character than to actually win them over on the merits of the best policies. We went for anger. But when was the last time any of us made a good decision based on anger? (Whether Kirsten Gillibrand at batting practice or me in the back of the House chamber fuming at President Obama, it's just not productive.)

Taking time to build relationships is one way through this mess. I was fortunate to learn this as a rookie state legislator in Pierre—when Larry invited me out for Chinese food with Matt, Jim, and Tim. Building relationships with those who disagree with me is something I've had to work at in public life, and goodness knows I'm not perfect at it. But I'm convinced it's a better way.

Chapter 16

Heading Home

Crazy as it may sound, it's easy to get comfortable in Congress. While the shock over the routine dysfunction and double-talk never really wears off, you *do* get used to all the frantic activity, the late-night votes, the reporters and lobbyists clamoring outside your office. If you're not careful, you can actually start to *like* all that attention. I noticed many of my colleagues on the Hill felt this made them important, when really it was the trust of their constituents back home that made them matter.

At the same time, serving in Congress means you're one of 435 members, so unless you're in a leadership role—as a committee chair, or majority leader, or Speaker of the House—your individual ability to make a difference is pretty limited. This is by design, and it's a mark of the wisdom of our country's Founders, but that doesn't make it any less frustrating if you're someone who likes to get things done.

Put all this together, and you get a weird environment: working in Washington makes you feel at the "center of it all," but at the same time you have little control and it's fairly easy to dodge responsibility when things go wrong.

Throughout our history, our best leaders never fell for the line that the federal government was the source of our strength or goodness. And as I neared the end of my third term in Congress, I became convinced that the best antidote for a Beltway mentality was getting back home. I could have stayed in a comfortable seat in Congress, probably for the rest of my life. But I don't like comfortable. And as the 2016 election season began, I had begun to feel it might be time to choose the hard way again. I still wanted to make a difference, but maybe it was time to do good for South Dakota *in* South Dakota.

And there was one great job for doing that: governor.

But 2016 was a presidential year, and there was so much more at stake for South Dakotans than just my seat in Congress. In the face of an increasingly liberal and aggressive national Democrat Party, there was a real feeling that our values and our very livelihood would be in the crosshairs if liberals were to tighten their grip on the federal government.

In that environment, I couldn't abandon my post.

Over her long and ruthless political career, Hillary Clinton had proved time and time again that she did not care about the rural way of life. She did not care to protect middle-class freedoms. She did not recognize the importance of Main Street businesses. Worst of all, she did not value American farmers. South Dakota is home to all of those things. Under a president like Hillary Clinton, we would have been in big trouble.

Donald Trump was something different. The New Yorker knew where the food for the cities came from. He was also a *fighter*: he was willing to fix what was broken and put conservative principles in place for families and businesses. And he loved America.

The national presidential campaign was full of ups and downs, but one of the worst moments came when the famous *Access Hollywood* video came out. We called it "Billy Bush weekend." In all honesty, I was shocked by what it contained, but I also never wavered in my belief that Donald Trump would still be a better president for the interests of South Dakota than Hillary Clinton.

At the time, I was the only woman among South Dakota's statewide officeholders. When I was the only one who didn't call for Donald Trump to drop out of the race immediately, the press came after me with a vengeance. It was a firestorm, but, luckily, the rest of the nation saw in Donald Trump what I saw. Against all odds, Donald Trump became the forty-fifth president of the United States, securing 306 electoral votes.

My own challenger in 2016, Paula Hawks, was a truly tough opponent. Personally, we actually had a lot in common: We'd both grown up on farms, earned degrees at South

Dakota State, and served in the state legislature before deciding to run for Congress. We also both lost a parent far too
early. Politically, however, we were exact opposites.

Fortunately, I had built a strong record over six years in
Congress as a hard, honest worker who kept her promises.
Most of all, though, I shared South Dakotans' commonsense
conservatism, and I believe that is why our campaign won so
big that year. When the race was called, I was reelected with
more than 64 percent of the vote.

When the presidential race was called that night, it felt
like a weight of doubt was lifted off our shoulders. Everybody
could breathe again knowing that South Dakotans were not
going to be left in the dust. Hope for America had been
restored. We all celebrated. Honestly, it was hard not to.

For me, there was also a sense of personal relief. I could
return home now and do so confident that South Dakotans
had a champion in the White House.

By my way of thinking, when it comes to deciding whether
to run for an office, there is only one right way to do it: as a
family.

Now, I'm very much a "go with my gut" person, but I
never wanted to run roughshod into something, dragging
Bryon and the kids along after me. From the time I started
in politics, we have made every big decision as a family, and
my run for governor was no different. Because we knew this
race would be different from anything else we'd ever done,

we needed more concrete information. We chose to poll the race over several days and then decide.

As always, it was more complicated than getting some numbers and seeing if there was any prayer of my becoming South Dakota's first woman governor. For starters, money was an issue. If I wanted to use the remaining funds in my federal campaign account for a 2018 gubernatorial run, state law required that I transfer the money before a deadline. That deadline was just a few days away. The problem was that the poll results weren't back yet.

As it turned out, I got the results of the poll the *day of the deadline* and had less than two hours to come to a decision, film an announcement video, and make the transfer while state law would still allow it.

That day, I drove to Sioux Falls to meet with some trusted members of our team and get the poll results. Bryon couldn't come, but he was ready for a call just as soon as we knew what we were up against.

Walking into the cool executive conference room down-town, I sensed the electricity in the air right away, almost like you can when a big storm is coming over the prairie. The team members were seated around a long table, and every single one of them was watching my face. Everyone knew I hated polling, and they were all trying to figure out how stressed I was about this particular poll.

We started the call and got right to business.

It was not good.

Essentially, if the race were held that day, I would have

lost the primary by eight points and the general election by six. While South Dakotans were more than comfortable electing a woman to represent them way far away in Washington, DC, attitudes were different when it came to that same woman serving as CEO of their state.

"No way. Or at least, not yet," someone said. "Your gender is definitely a factor."

The call ended, and I looked around the room. No one said anything.

I pushed myself away from the table. "Let me call Bryon."

Bryon answered on the first ring: "Well, how does it look?"

Bryon had never been thrilled to have me halfway across the country five days a week. Compared to DC, the governor's mansion in Pierre was practically down the street.

I filled him in on the polling, and he grew quiet.

"What do you think?" he asked after a moment.

I thought of what Bryon had told me more than once: *You always choose the hardest way.*

"I think we do it anyway," I answered. "And I think we'll win. But if we don't, then I'll be home."

"Okay, let's do it," Bryon replied immediately.

We hung up.

I walked back into the conference room and all eyes landed on mine.

"We're running."

When the team stopped cheering, we made a few quick additional decisions surrounding an announcement and then filed out to get to work. It felt good to have the decision made, but we all knew this coming race would be harder than anything else we'd achieved. The first congressional run against Stephanie Herseth Sandlin was going to look easy by comparison given what we now knew about the landscape. I mentioned earlier how the tension surrounding the decision had reminded me of a storm coming across the prairie.

Little did any of us know just how big that storm would be.

The next day, I released a video announcing my bid for governor.

It had been just six days since I'd won reelection to the US House of Representatives, and immediately my decision drew a lot of criticism. People said I "jumped the gun." Others argued I'd be too preoccupied with what was going on with the campaign back home to serve effectively in Washington. Others even accused me of doing a disservice to the people of South Dakota, claiming that I was "abandoning my post" right when we finally got a promising leader in the White House. Given how much thought I had put into the decision, this last critique was really rich. But that's what you sign up for in politics: having people misunderstand your motives, and too often seeing others fan those flames of misunderstanding on purpose.

In the end, you simply have to trust your own decision. I was grateful South Dakotans had trusted me to represent them in Congress. And I was excited to spend my last two years working with President Trump on the big issues of the day, especially tax reform. But I never doubted my choice to come home. I had run for Congress to find conservative solutions and make a difference for South Dakota and the country. I was not there to make a career out of it.

And truth be told, there was work that needed to be done in South Dakota. The Republican legislators and governors who came before me got a lot of things right, but more and more of our young people were starting to leave, and that's never a good sign. Our future depended on our ability to honestly evaluate where we were and make tough choices necessary to create new opportunities for families and small businesses. The rising generation of South Dakotans needed the opportunity to not just survive but *thrive* in their home state, to find rewarding careers and raise their children surrounded by family and friends in communities that solved problems together.

It was time for fresh ideas from someone who had to hustle to make a dollar and stretch that dollar to make it last. I had the business and policy experience that people needed in Pierre, and I was ready and able to get to work from day one.

The country and the state had just come through a grueling campaign season, and everyone—my family included—needed a break from politics. The timing of my announcement wasn't perfect. But that's the thing—there's never "a perfect time." I needed the people to know that I would do whatever I could to take South Dakota to the next level.

They needed to know, from that moment on, I was all in.

*   *   *

When I announced my decision to run for governor, there were already two Republicans in the race, then nearly two years away. One was South Dakota's attorney general, Marty Jackley. The other was Mark Mickelson, a Sioux Falls lawyer and Speaker of the state house. Mark came from a prominent political family in South Dakota, and you could say being governor was in his blood: both his father and his grandfather had served as our state's chief executive. (Tragically, Mark's father died in a plane crash while in office in 1993.) Jackley and Mickelson were both well respected. A primary between them would be a tough fight—and I had dropped myself right into the middle of it.

South Dakota may be small in population and our people may be peaceful by nature, but like any other place, our politics can still be pretty nasty. The hard truth is South Dakota had—and still has—a bit of what you might call a "good ol' boys' club," and that club typically handpicked the candidate for governor.

Spoiler alert: in 2018, that candidate was not me.

But one Sunday morning in early November 2016, just a few days after I had announced for the race, I received another one of those life-changing phone calls. It was from Mark, and it was a call that I was as shocked to receive as he probably was to make.

Mark was thinking of getting out of the race. He asked if we could meet.

I said yes.

I had always respected Mark; he was a good friend and an even better leader in the legislature, where he was known for being tough but fair. But our conversation that Sunday revealed another one of Mark's qualities, one that is sadly all too rare in politics: humility. In the end, I told Mark if he was offering it, I would be honored to have his support in the race.

Looking back now, I realize that call must have been even tougher for Mark to make than I understood at the time. Conviction runs deep in my own heart. My father was a farmer, and I don't think I could ever walk away from agriculture completely. Mark's father had been *governor*, but here he was choosing to let it go because he knew it wasn't right for him at this time. To this day, I am in awe of that self-awareness and willingness to act on it.

Sometimes, we cast longer shadows than we know, and it's important to be aware of the pressure that can put on our kids. Letting them find their own way in life can be hard, especially since we only want the best for them. But I'm convinced it's a fundamental part of loving them.

That 2018 governor's race was a like a knife fight in a ditch. Even after Mark withdrew, the primary with Jackley was bitterly divisive. While I ultimately won by twelve points, some Republican stalwarts ended up working against me in the general election. To make matters tougher, the Democrats had a strong candidate in Billie Sutton—a seasoned member of the state senate and a former professional bronc rider. (A less advertised fact about him is he was also a firm Bernie Sanders supporter.)

The general election was a tight race. Every day, I had to dig down deep and get up to fight for one more inch of ground. There were some good days; there were a lot more hard days.

One night, Bryon, Kennedy, and I pulled into Webster, a small town in the northeastern corner of South Dakota, to watch Booker play football. I had spent all day at campaign events and had just gotten some bad news by phone. As Bryon parked, I explained the situation while he and Kennedy listened. I told Bryon to go ahead to the stands for the kickoff, and that I would be right there. As he got out of the pickup and shut the door, I laid my head back and started to cry.

Kennedy sat silently for a minute in the backseat. Then, in a quiet but firm voice my daughter said, "Mom, don't you think God is *exhausted* from us doubting Him all the time?"

That hit me. Hard. If I was really going to say I had faith in God, then I needed to act like it. I dried my tears, put on a smile, and we went to cheer on my son at his game.

The 2018 governor's race ranks as one of the most arduous experiences of my life. I had to call Kennedy's words to mind *every day* simply to get through it. Along the way, I learned much more than I ever expected about building a team. One key lesson: put people in positions where they can be successful, then trust them to deliver.

In the end, we won by three points. It was the closest gubernatorial race in South Dakota in thirty years. Considering we began the campaign running six points *behind*, the final result was a testament to hard work—and trust.

Difficult though it was, of the many choices I have made since entering politics, leaving Congress to come home to South Dakota remains the best.

Chapter 17

A Hard Year

Remember, Kristi," my friend Beth Hollatz told me right after my election as governor. "You have priorities, but we have no control over what the good Lord sends our way. And we don't always know the reason."

I've known Beth for decades now. She was one of the first people to encourage me to run for public office, and she has been a stalwart friend and counselor at every step. She was a second mother to our kids when I was away in DC—even going so far as to bathe horses at rodeos with my girls when I wasn't there to do it. I respect Beth endlessly, so when she spoke these words to me, I paid attention.

Beth and her husband ran a family restaurant together in Clark, South Dakota, for more than twenty years. Restaurants are a tough business, with tight profit margins. I figured if anybody knew about getting thrown a few curveballs, it was Beth. And while her words apply to any line of work, I've found they're especially true when that work happens to be serving as governor of your state.

You need a vision and the energy to make that vision real, but you must also realize things will come up that you never expected. Some will be good. Plenty will be not so good. And some will be truly awful. But you can't complain about it. That's just the job. Being in charge doesn't always mean being in control, after all, but it *does* mean being accountable for fixing things when they go wrong. This demands humility, resilience, and faith.

And grit.

Because when those curveballs come at you, you can't whiff. People put their trust in you. They're counting on you. Preparing for the inauguration, I promised myself I wasn't going to let hard realities keep me from delivering on the priorities of South Dakotans. And while I believe I've kept that promise, little did I know just how many of life's unexpected realities were headed my way.

It all began very symbolically. November 2018 marked the centennial of women's suffrage in South Dakota, and I had just been elected the state's first woman governor. So the significance of my swearing-in was lost on no one. To honor those early suffragettes, I decided to order a white suit for the ceremony in the state capitol rotunda and a dress with purple colors for the evening ball later that night. Of course, the suit didn't arrive in time, so I ended up wearing a boring black pantsuit that had been hanging in my closet for years.

I was sworn in on my dad's Bible, which I had kept on my desk during my time in Congress. Swearing the oath, with Bryon standing beside me, I was overcome with gratitude and awe. We were just a little farm family, after all. At the end of the day, we relied on God and the dirt for our livelihood, like everyone else in South Dakota.

Yet there we were.

After the ceremony, there was a reception, and we served everyone my favorite ice cream: Dairy Queen's chocolate-covered strawberry blizzards.

"Blizzards!" someone joked. "How fitting for South Dakota!"

We laughed.

They were more fitting than anybody knew.

"Why doesn't anybody *talk*?" I asked in exasperation.

My acting chief of staff, Herb Jones, and I had just left our daily team meeting and were walking the hallway back to my office in the state capitol. A former chief of staff for John Thune, Herb had been instrumental on the campaign trail, and I'd asked him to stay on for an interim period before he left to work in social services.

That morning, our footsteps were probably louder than usual on the terrazzo tiles: I'm a fast walker in general, but

I was frustrated today. The legislature had been in session for three weeks, which meant we were halfway through. In South Dakota, the session is short—only about forty days—and the governor's staff meets daily to discuss the bills that have been filed and their potential impact.

Only there wasn't much discussion happening at all.

The staff members attending our daily meetings were staying quiet. As much as we tried to encourage those in the room to talk, the dialogue never became a debate. Which meant I couldn't get the full picture.

As we arrived at my office, Josh, another senior member of my team, walked in to overhear the conversation.

"I don't understand," I said to Herb and Josh. "I keep trying to get them to speak up. Do they think I have all the answers? Why don't they say something?!"

Josh was quiet for a moment. Then he sighed. "Why don't you try being quiet for a while?"

I stopped. "What do you mean?" I asked defensively.

"Listen," he said. "Whenever we bring up a new topic, you're pretty quick to state your opinion. And no one wants to argue with the governor. So why don't you try being quiet for a while? Let them debate it before you speak, so they feel more free to share their opinions."

The next day, I did exactly that.

It worked.

The more it became clear that I was listening, the more confident my staff became. They began to share more details and air differing views. I got more information that morning than I'd gotten in three weeks.

Proverbs 18:2 states "A fool takes no pleasure in understanding, but only in expressing his opinion" (ESV). It was a humbling lesson for me—one I was glad to learn early in office.

New governors often enjoy what's called "a honeymoon phase." That may be, but I didn't want to waste any time basking in it. The first bill I signed was for constitutional carry to protect South Dakotans' Second Amendment rights. A few weeks into the session, I unveiled my proposed budget. In early February 2019, I traveled to Connecticut to commission the USS *South Dakota*—the Navy's newest, most technologically advanced nuclear attack submarine.

So far, so good, I remember thinking. *No curveballs yet.*

Because I wanted to begin a new relationship of reconciliation between the Native American tribes and South Dakota's state government, I invited each to hang a tribal flag in our state capitol's rotunda to honor them and remind everyone of their important role in both our state's history and our future. I wanted to build a solid foundation in helping them address serious challenges—poverty, lack of quality health care, addiction, and crime. It wouldn't be easy, but it was going to be a priority.

I was feeling fairly confident. This wasn't my first rodeo, and so far, little had come our way that I hadn't expected. That was about to change.

*   *   *

In March 2019, two masses of warm and cold air met in the skies above the central United States. A sudden, steep drop in pressure created an incredibly powerful weather system that stretched from Texas to North Dakota. It was known by meteorologists as a bomb cyclone. That name was appropriate.

On Monday, March 11, the team was gathered in my office, waiting for the different committees to reach agreement on the final budget, when we got the first call about an approaching winter storm called Ulmer.

South Dakotans are no strangers to harsh weather. We're taught from an early age to respect nature as something life-giving, but also powerful and dangerous and far outside our ability to control. (People still talk about the tragic "Children's Blizzard" of 1888, when snow as fine as flour and frigid temperatures blew in so suddenly that many children who had been dismissed early from school froze to death before they could reach home.)

As we left the capitol that night, the air had that heavy feeling to it, and we knew to expect snow. It had been forecasted for days. With the final budget negotiations over and the session's work wrapped up in the early morning hours, many legislators headed for home to beat the storm. Others hunkered down in town to wait it out.

Over the next forty-eight hours, winter storm Ulmer delivered our first unexpected reality.

With wind gusts reaching 70 mph, the storm buried western and central South Dakota under five feet of heavy, wet snow. Nearly two hundred miles of Interstate 90, the highway connecting both halves of our state, was closed. In Pierre, the wind speed rapidly climbed into blizzard territory, blowing snow to form waist-high drifts down the city streets and making the roads utterly impassable. On the eastern side of the state, six inches of rain fell in a matter of hours. That rain fell on frozen ground—and soon roared south in gushing torrents. Roads washed out. Dams burst. *Everything* flooded.

In the storm's immediate aftermath, I was eager to get out to the hardest-hit communities. Where the governor goes, the attention and resources of the state follow, and I knew some of our more isolated communities would need lots of help—fast. But getting out of Pierre proved impossible. Snowplows were struggling through walls of heavy snow; airports and runways were still snowed in.

So I walked—first to the emergency operations center, where the state's incredibly dedicated team was assembling to field requests for help and route resources, then to the hospital to make sure there were enough supplies to care for their current patients. By this time, the snow was so high, the kids and I had to shovel to get the front door of the governor's residence open, and it was slow going as we pushed our way through drifts that came up to my waist. Between meetings, I checked in with local businesses to see how people were doing. More than a few times I had to assure people that the soggy, shivering woman coming in from the snow was in fact the governor.

All federal aid requests from across the state would be filed and coordinated through the ops center, and I knew our people would be working around the clock responding to needs across South Dakota, documenting every action taken so federal reimbursement could be coordinated where appropriate. People in Pierre seemed stable, but I was still worried about those isolated communities.

I decided to mobilize the National Guard. I also asked for one of the Black Hawk helicopters stationed at Rapid City to take me to the areas being threatened by rising floodwaters.

Ulmer had hit those towns hard, and water was the biggest problem—too much and not enough. Too much because bridges and roads had washed out. Not enough because with all the topsoil washed away, pipes were collapsing and residents couldn't get clean drinking water.

One of the first actions we took was to establish swift water rescue task forces to evacuate people stranded by flash floods. We coordinated with local, state, and federal agencies to reestablish clean drinking water. We dispatched the National Guard to wherever they were needed.

I spent weeks traveling our state, learning the unique needs of each community and getting help and assistance to them right away. I quickly learned that clearing and repaving roads was a major priority. In many places on our reservations, the roads were federally maintained. This meant, for liability reasons, the state couldn't repair them ourselves. It was maddening to be prevented by law from simply doing the job ourselves, but we did what we could. We helped with barriers and provided law enforcement to help divert traffic until repairs could be made.

Winter storm Wesley hit South Dakota less than one month later, on April 16. More snow. More driving rain. More devastation. This time, the floodwaters threatened not only those living in remote and isolated parts of the state, but also those residing in our major cities.

In Sioux Falls, the Big Sioux River winds its way through the heart of the city. When it breaches its banks, the damage can be catastrophic. The people of Sioux Falls were well prepared, but state resources were also necessary to protect lives and prevent as much damage as possible.

April 16 marked my one hundredth day as governor. It had been a very different first hundred days than what I had imagined. In the first quarter of 2019 alone, sixty-three of our sixty-six counties were declared federal disaster areas— some multiple times over.

Then came the tornadoes.

On August 6, the city of Burke was hit by a category F1. Hail more than three inches in diameter fell across the town. Homes and businesses were destroyed. The twister also toppled legacy trees, ripping their roots out of soil softened by all the moisture the area had received over the previous months. Many of these trees fell in ways that crushed everything around them—yet, miraculously, did not take any lives. Again, I mobilized the National Guard and traveled to

Burke myself to help with the response. Walking its streets, I could stare straight into school classrooms and living rooms. In one house, I saw a glass coffee table sitting entirely undisturbed, while the world had been torn apart around it.

One month after that, on the evening of September 10, three tornadoes hit Sioux Falls, wiping out businesses, homes, and hospitals all on the same night. Once again, South Dakota's first responders sprang into action. While devastating, it was fortunate that the tornadoes had come at night: most of the businesses were closed and empty of people.

With every new set of storms came new waves of rainfall and new flooding. Across South Dakota, people had spent months coping with the havoc by driving miles and miles around washed-out roads to get to work, the grocery store, or the doctor. There are no tougher people than South Dakotans, but I could tell they were getting tired.

On September 12, the sixty-five hundred people of the city of Madison were threatened by new floodwaters. Projections indicated the most vulnerable areas; a nursing home and a residential neighborhood were right in the flood path. I spoke with local leaders who were considering building a levee across a state highway to divert the waters around the town. Throughout our conversations, it became clear we couldn't predict what the impact of such a diversion would be. By solving one problem, we might cause an even bigger problem down the line. I spent hours with local leaders working to find the best solution.

In the end, we decided to evacuate.

When I arrived in Madison, I found a sight that was by now familiar and so inspiring: friends and families working alongside one another, encouraging one another, telling stories to keep their spirits high. They were dealing with a hard reality, packing up their families and belongings. They were uniting to support each other as a community. They were doing what South Dakotans do best.

As we battled nature all through 2019, repairing roads and bridges before the fall harvest became a top priority. Farmers would be struggling to get their crops harvested out of muddy fields. Finding roads solid enough to handle heavy trucks would be difficult. I also knew crop yields would be low from all the flooding. On top of everything else, there would be financial hardship and the all-consuming worry that comes with it.

In December, I released my budget for the coming year. The dreadful storms and floods of 2019 had taken a toll not only on our physical and mental health, but also on the state's fiscal health. We would need to backfill our emergency funds and put money into our Infrastructure Disaster Recovery Fund to rebuild. I proposed a conservative revenue forecast, recognizing agriculture as our number one industry. When agriculture struggles, every business in the state struggles. Since our major source of state funding is a 4.5 percent sales tax, we would need to prepare for people having less money to spend because of the hardships of 2019.

Looking back on that first year, it seems there were entire days when we did nothing but fill sandbags. I worked alongside volunteers and prisoners, emergency first responders and grandparents, schoolkids and parents. You learn about the people who work side by side with you in situations like that. You understand more deeply the people of the area you call your home. What I will say is this: South Dakotans have iron bones—we don't break. We also have big hearts. There is no one you'd rather have with you when times get tough.

Throughout 2019, I often thought of the song "Oceans" by Hillsong. If you're not familiar, it talks about grace abounding in the deepest waters, how in turbulent times, trust in God is key. Sometimes, that faith leads us to answers. Sometimes, it just reminds us that God walks with us through our pain. And pain is an opportunity to grow—and grow *stronger* for whatever lies ahead.

As 2019 closed, we'd had enough unexpected realities for one year. Everyone was just glad to get 2019 behind us and welcome the new year of 2020. Surely, things could only get better.

Chapter 18

Tribal Trials

Don't waste your time going to the reservations; they will never vote for you."

It was in 2010 during my first congressional race when an elected official spoke these words to me. The cynicism was jaw-dropping, and I went to the reservations anyway.

I knew South Dakota's tribes historically voted for Democrats, but completely ignoring them while seeking to represent all of South Dakota was not acceptable to me. What's more, no true public servant, of any party, could rightly ignore the problems facing the Native communities: overwhelming unemployment and chronic poverty, violent crime, rampant alcohol and drug addiction, and, most heartbreaking, child suicide.

I'm not naive enough to think that any one person—in government or outside it—can solve these problems. But one person of goodwill can find another, and those two can find more like them. And *that* group can absolutely make a difference.

As a public servant, my guiding principle on tribal issues has been simple: *Let me try.*

French fur trappers first arrived in what became South Dakota in the 1740s. That may seem like a long time ago for most, but Native Americans had been living in the area nearly ten thousand years by that time. Today, South Dakota is home to the Lakota, Nakota, and Dakota people. In the time since the first white settlers appeared, our shared history has been a painful one of broken promises, violence, death, and neglect. Growing up I learned a little about those interactions, but not nearly enough—and certainly not in context.

The Lakota don't write down their history. They share it orally through stories told over and over so the rising generation will remember. For their children to truly understand the past, they must hear and feel deeply the victories, defeats, and heartbreaks of their elders. This deep emotional and spiritual bond between generations is what preserves the culture and guarantees its survival. These stories and this bond are also inextricably tied to the land, and the spiritual center of the Lakota people is in the Black Hills. That is where their dead are buried.

The Treaty of Fort Laramie in 1868 had promised the Black Hills would belong to the Indians forever, but that treaty was never honored by the US government. This broken promise made the completion of Mount Rushmore in 1941 even harder to bear: not only did the white men steal Lakota land, but they then carved the mountain into the images of *their* leaders.

In response, in 1948, Lakota chief Henry Standing Bear commissioned sculptor Korczak Ziolkowski to carve a separate mountain in the Black Hills as a memorial honoring the great leader of the Lakota tribe, Crazy Horse. Standing Bear and his fellow chiefs had watched the construction of Mount Rushmore come to fruition and wanted a memorial to their own Indigenous hero. Sadly, that project has yet to be completed today.

Crazy Horse is revered as a brave, compassionate leader who always put his people first. He wisely knew in his heart that his people's greatest need was freedom, and he led them to some of the greatest victories the Lakota had ever known. His own death was tragic: after surrendering to the US Army to keep his people safe, he was arrested on the basis of a rumor and, in the ensuing struggle, bayoneted. Today, Crazy Horse has a legacy as a leader never captured and never defeated in battle. And it is all the more powerful that one of his last requests on behalf of his people was "I want to keep our sacred Black Hills."

Native Americans long for reconciliation. They want an acknowledgment and apology for the mistreatment of the tribes. And an apology feels hollow unless it leads to some measure of healing and agreement on the path forward toward a new relationship. The hard part is finding agreement on what is an acceptable restitution and restoration. The Lakota, Nakota, and Dakota tribes want the Black Hills returned to them. They have rejected restitution for the land and it has been difficult to find another alternative. The difficulty in returning the land to the tribe and the legal challenges such an action would present seem nearly impossible to navigate. The mistrust and bitterness of past generations still exist today.

But I believe we must find a path forward, and I've worked to find one ever since entering public life. This has caused some pretty big controversies among tribal leaders and in certain political circles in South Dakota. For starters, there's a ridiculous stereotype that "Republicans aren't supposed to care about the plight of Native Americans." I flatly reject that. I *do* care. And I simply wasn't going to stand by and do nothing.

Once in Congress, I discovered that while I could champion individual projects for South Dakota's tribes, it was almost impossible to bring about larger, systemic change. Progress was too easily stalled in a chamber of 435. As governor, I tried a different approach.

During the 2018 campaign, I didn't promise miracles—I was under no illusions that centuries of hard history could be brushed aside—but I did express my desire to find even just one tribe that was willing to work with me. New government-to-government relationships were key.

Within a couple of months of taking office, I began making regular trips to the Pine Ridge Indian Reservation—to meet with community leaders. To talk. The tribe's president was not interested in meeting with me, much less in working together. Several times, he did not show up for our scheduled meetings at tribal headquarters. Often, he was unexpectedly out of town. After a few months, I took a different approach—I began coordinating directly with individuals on specific issues.

One evening in 2019, I arrived at dusk in Wounded Knee, the community defined by the horrible massacre of nearly three hundred Lakota people by soldiers of the United States Army on December 29, 1890. It had been a long day meeting with families, but there was one person I still had to see. Tom Hollow Horn was a Lakota man who had been asking me to visit for a particular purpose: to see an empty building in the community that he wanted to turn into a youth center. Tom needed funding, and he hoped I could help him.

The day of my visit, I had been unable to reach Tom by phone. I didn't know where he lived, and I didn't know where this building was. But I was going to try to find both.

As we drove into the community, I felt the heaviness of Wounded Knee's history. The women, children, and men who died defenseless that day were a testimony to the grave injustices suffered by the Lakota. It is impossible for me to reconcile the event in my heart. It grieves me even now when

I think of it; a darkness settles on my spirit whenever I do. How could I restore even the slightest measure of trust, even after so many years?

There had still been no word from Tom, but as we drove, I saw a man walking up a dirt trail to a cluster of houses. "Let's head over that way," I said to my security detail. "Maybe he knows where the building is."

My driver reluctantly turned up the dirt trail after the man, but as we approached, he began to walk faster. I leaned out the window and called after him—and he broke out into a run. It hit me then: being followed by a black Suburban is unsettling for anyone, but here at Wounded Knee it had an even worse connotation. We needed to back off.

We turned around and began driving around the area, hoping to find this empty building that Tom referred to in our conversations. Everywhere we looked we saw heartbreak: houses without doors and with broken windows, litter filling the ditches, kids playing in abandoned lots among rusted-out cars, and dogs roaming everywhere.

I could sense my security detail getting nervous, but I was determined to find Tom.

As night fell, we finally located what we thought was the potential youth center, at the top of a steep hill. Shining our headlights on the doors, we saw they were secured with a log chain and padlock. We were standing outside the vehicle talking about what to do next, when suddenly several vehicles came roaring up the hill, the lights blinding us as they came to an abrupt stop. Doors slammed. Dust swirled. There was shouting.

"Kristi! Kristi! You made it!"

A warm face and wrinkled hand came out from the headlights and greeted me with excitement. Suddenly, I was surrounded by curious gazes. We had been looking for him, but Tom had found us.

"It doesn't look like we can get in, Tom," I told him after we all exchanged greetings. "It's locked."

Even in the dark, I could see Tom's face fall when he realized no one in the group had the key. Worse, he didn't know who had locked the building, which meant he didn't know where we could find a key. Maybe we couldn't get a tour, but at least Tom could tell me his vision for the center.

A few minutes into his explanation, we suddenly heard the clang of chains dropping.

A young woman's voice came out of the dark: "Hey, I got it unlocked. You can come in now."

To this day, I have no idea how that young woman got past those heavy chains. But there in the dark at Wounded Knee, my mind instantly went back to that night at the rodeo grounds in 2010, when I smashed out the windows of our horse trailer so Kassidy could make her competition on time. It dawned on me: I had been searching for some way to bridge the divide between my heritage and those of the Lakota people, and this young woman had just shown it. Neither of us had hesitated to break a barrier if it led to helping those we loved.

This is how we go forward, I thought.

The building was filled with garbage, rats, and dirt, but Tom showed me around with optimism. He could see the potential, and as he spoke I could too. The people with him told me stories of the children in the community who had nowhere safe to go to do homework or spend time outside of school. They spoke of broken homes, addiction, abuse. More than once Tom's eyes filled with tears as he told these stories. But there was also pride—and hope. Tom had dreams for this center. And he wasn't alone in that. A couple of the young men with him had composed a rap, and they performed it for us right there in the dilapidated building. As I listened, I was overwhelmed with an urge to help this crew.

When it was time to leave, we loaded up after a round of hugs and left with a promise to see what we could do to work together. I was hopeful. A community center was a good start. It was tangible—real. But while we had overcome a padlock and chain, none of us could have guessed the barrier that was about to be dropped in front of us.

The Pine Ridge Reservation in southwest South Dakota comprises more than two million acres—larger than some East Coast states. The geographic isolation of most reservations means economic development is difficult. Landownership issues limit investment, and educational opportunities are lacking. These problems are compounded by the daily challenges of addiction and violence. These are unique challenges, to be sure, but nothing is impossible if you have determined people of goodwill.

A short time after our meeting with Tom, I went back to Pine Ridge to meet with the community about youth programs and leadership training, but this time, some local leaders had invited the civil rights activist and community development expert Bob Woodson to come with me. Bob had traveled to South Dakota specifically for this visit. His work in community development in hard-hit urban centers throughout America has resulted in amazing transformations in some of the country's most challenged communities. Pine Ridge, South Dakota, may be about as different from some of those cities as you can get, but I believed Bob could give us some insight and guidance on how our tribal communities could turn things around.

We had invited the president of the tribe and the entire tribal council to attend this gathering at the community center, but not one of them came. I was disappointed, but we started the discussion with Bob anyway. Thanks to his help, we were soon holding an honest conversation about past hurts, and what we could do to heal and move forward.

At one point, a young man stood up before the group.

"Governor Noem," he began, "I hear many bad things about you ... and I believe them. But you are starting to show up so often now, that I am beginning to believe that you really do care."

Most people would say that wasn't a glowing endorsement; however, I treasured his words: They were the first real sign of progress. There was hope.

*   *   *

Days after this last visit to Pine Ridge, a press release went out from tribal headquarters and the Office of the President of the Oglala Sioux Tribe, Julian Bear Runner: I had been prohibited from returning to the reservation. The stated reason was my support for two bills in the legislature relating to the Keystone XL. I understand tribal leaders see the issue through a lens of respect for the earth and sovereignty—and a long history of false promises. But given the timing, I believe the prohibition had more to do with my showing up and having real conversations with families on the reservation.

What if I just went anyway? I remember thinking to myself when I first began reading the letter. The tribe must have anticipated that, because one sentence answered my thought directly: "If you do not honor this directive—for example, if you were to repeat your recent visit absent permission from our tribal government—we will have no choice but to banish you."

Frustrated does not even begin to describe how I felt. It was clear to me then: Those in charge feared a change of heart and attitude from tribal communities toward a governor who genuinely cared about bringing change. They feared a loss of influence. Yet, despite my own feelings, I knew the history: promises had been made to the tribes so many times before, and so many times those promises had been broken. *Would I feel any differently if I were in their shoes?*

Out of respect for the tribe, I honored the letter. And in no uncertain terms it has hurt my ability to grow the relationships so crucial to making real progress for tribal families. The truth is that progress cannot happen without trust, and trust can come only from time spent together. Once trust is established, you can have the honest, organic conversations that explore solutions without pride or prejudice. This was exactly what we had begun doing. This was exactly what the tribal leaders shut down.

Some, I am sure, believe it was naive of me to spend so much time working on tribal issues. At first glance, they may seem right: since spring 2019, restrictions on my visiting the reservations have been lifted and put back into place. When necessary, I have continued my engagement from afar, with limited progress.

The problems facing America's tribal communities are deep and complex, and in South Dakota, the hard truth is that Democrat politicians and Lakota tribal leaders have solved none of them. The politically expedient thing for Republicans is to simply walk away, and I cannot do that. These are our fellow Americans; however heartbreaking our past chapters may have been, we are part of the same story. And we have a long way to go before that story changes from a narrative of tragedy and despair to one of hope and fulfillment. True reconciliation will not happen until we learn to take a chance on doing things differently than we have in the past. That means meeting with arms uncrossed and eyes wide open. That has been my stance, and that will remain my stance.

I know now what I should have said to that elected official back in 2010, the one who told me not to bother going to the reservations because they'd never vote for me: *I am more interested in working with our tribes to enact change to help and give hope than I am in securing more votes.*

Chapter 19

Girl Talk

If you've stayed with me this far, you know I regard my time growing up on a working farm as the single most significant preparation I had for serving as governor. Funny though it may sound, the *second*-most-significant experience—and it is, admittedly, a distant second—was the year I spent as South Dakota Snow Queen. I say that with complete sincerity.

Okay, so what is a Snow Queen?

Initiated in 1947, the South Dakota Snow Queen competition is a scholarship program for high school girls. Local chapters host competitions where entrants are assessed on character and how well they promote South Dakota values, like hard work and personal responsibility. The winners go on to compete at an annual event in Aberdeen, South Dakota. The lucky girl who is named Snow Queen then spends a year promoting South Dakota and its people, industry, history, and values at a range of different events across the state. Public speaking is a big part of it.

In 1990, I was a farm kid who did the same thing every other senior girl did, only when I competed in my local competition, I happened to win. Surprised, I went on to the state competition and before I knew it, there I was: Snow Queen. Yours truly received a scholarship to use at a college of my choice, as well as the use of a car for one year. (I wrecked it, and as far as I know, that was the last year the program organizers gifted the winner a car.)

But I got to travel around as an ambassador for South Dakota. I gave speeches and interviews, and, looking back, it was all surprisingly similar to what I do now as governor. If I'm being honest, I was awkward at it back then. Occasionally, I still feel awkward at it today. But as I tell young people now—especially young girls—you must decide you're going to be a teachable person. This means you must be comfortable being uncomfortable, willing to try something new, and maybe be awkward for a little while. If I hadn't all those years ago, I would never have learned a critical skill that's served me well ever since.

Since getting into politics, I've received a lot of requests to speak to young girls' groups. Whenever I do, I always encourage young women to put themselves forward and compete in whatever field they're in. You simply never know what may come from it—a new mentor, a new job, a new skill. Life is full of surprises, and plenty of them are good ones. The only sure mistake is to hang back because you don't know if you're somehow "enough." Trust me, you are.

As much as I give this advice, it's frustrating to find that so often the field young girls want to go into isn't a fair one. Certainly, I've known this to be true in politics. But increasingly this is becoming the case in girls' youth sports, as more and more biological males seek to compete as girls.

I competed in sports growing up. So did both of my daughters, one of whom earned a scholarship for it. Girls-only athletics taught them confidence, how to grow a skill, build discipline, and be a team player. They learned how to deal with disappointment and how to succeed graciously, and all the other things so many of us learn from sports.

For me, allowing biological boys to compete in all-girls sports isn't just a policy question. It's about fairness—and, yes, it's deeply personal. I believe it's deeply personal for millions of other moms out there too. Because what's the point of encouraging our girls to put themselves out there if society simply won't allow them to be successful?

Unlike most pundits who debate the issue now, I have protected girls' sports my entire political career, and I have real results to show for my work. In Congress, I fought back when bureaucrats in the US Department of Agriculture tried eliminating girls-only riding events in 4-H rodeos in 2018. I won. It's why we still have girls' rodeo events in South Dakota.

Early in 2021, South Dakota's legislature passed House Bill 1217—a bill that was supposed to protect girls' sports. Among other things, Republicans in the state legislature aimed to prevent biological males from competing in girls' sports. From the beginning, I applauded their efforts, and I promised to sign the bill.

But by the time it reached my desk, the bill had picked up a number of other provisions that I believed were extremely problematic. For example, the legislature included a section barring the use of "performance-enhancing drugs" among student athletes. Sounds good, at first. But the bill failed to define just what constituted "performance-enhancing drugs." Did it include the steroids found in inhalers used by children with asthma? What about young athletes who took a cortisone shot for a busted knee or shoulder? What about a child on attention deficit disorder medication, another common steroid? (Major League Baseball has been wrestling with this issue for several years now—they still haven't figured out how to precisely define the term.)

The legislation also included language allowing student athletes to sue schools and other students if, for example, they didn't make a sports team and it was later discovered another player had violated the undefined statute. Students could also pursue litigation if they lost a game—presumably against another child who may have been taking some undefined "performance-enhancing drug."

Worse, the bill's poorly drafted language almost guaranteed it would get hung up in the courts for years, and, as a

228

consequence, I would not be able to enforce girls-only play in girls' sports.

I told the legislature that I was eager to sign the bill for this reason, but they had to fix these issues. I was looking forward to signing the bill into law. For whatever reason, the bill's sponsors wound up refusing to make the changes I requested, and the bill died.

What a firestorm came my way then—from Republicans. But the same day the bill died in the legislature, I signed two executive orders. The first one directed that only biological girls could compete in girls' sports in our K–12 public school system. The second applied the same directive in our collegiate sports. These executive orders had no expiration date, and they remained in place until the legislature passed my air-tight bill to protect fairness in women's sports in early February 2022. The bill that I proposed and which the legislature passed is the strongest girls sports law in the nation.

At its most basic level, this was about fairness. Every young woman deserves an equal playing field where she can achieve success, but common sense tells us that males have an unfair physical advantage over females in athletic competition. (I'm pretty fit myself, but I'm never going to bench-press more than Bryon; it just isn't going to happen.) Because of that, only girls should be competing in girls' sports. It's really as simple as that.

I first ran for office in 2006. Since then, I've learned people treat you differently as a woman in politics. Is it fair?

Absolutely not. But I've learned you can either burn energy being angry at it, or you can focus on accomplishing what you set out to achieve for the people counting on you. Learn the business. Build the relationships. Outwork everybody else around you. And give the rest to God.

Chapter 20

Principles for a Pandemic

Real leadership is principled decision-making. You decide on a vision based on your principles and then make all the many decisions that will bring together the most capable people with the most accurate information to give it life.

Information is often the hardest ingredient to find, and you never have as much as you want. Rather than a roadmap, most times you get a mosaic—one with plenty of missing tiles. But whether you have a little information or a lot, *principle* is the light you walk by. And a leader must know his or her principles by heart long before any crisis comes.

I knew my principles for governing well before the global COVID-19 pandemic began in the spring of 2020:

Stay transparent.

Know government's true limits.

Trust the people.

I had governed by these values for fourteen months before the pandemic hit. Sadly, after March 2020, too many so-called leaders in Washington did not follow these concepts, or anything even remotely resembling them. And when the crisis came, as millions of Americans wrestled with their health, with debilitating fear and incredible personal loss, we saw how deep confusion over first principles makes a devastating situation even worse.

The year 2020 began as hopeful as any other. In my State of the State address in January, I declared South Dakota "Open for Business." Just because South Dakota's population is small, there was no reason we couldn't lead the country as a place to live, raise a family, work, or open a business. Going back to principles, I promised a respectful, humble state government that would help where it could—and get the heck out of the way where it couldn't. Specifically, I invited industrious Americans to come to South Dakota and start a business. In exchange, I promised our government would not punish them with mindless regulations, endless red tape, and heavy tax burdens.

But 2020 had other ideas. Two short months later, we learned nobody would be going anywhere anytime soon.

*   *   *

When Melissa Klemann, my senior health policy adviser, walked into my office that morning in March 2020, she wore a grim look on her face.

"What is it?" I asked.

Melissa had grown up on a ranch south of Highmore. She was tough, and there wasn't much that worried her. But Melissa was clearly concerned, and that worried *me*.

"The Department of Health has just confirmed South Dakota's first cases of COVID-19," Melissa said. She paused. "And we've already had our first death."

I felt my stomach drop. "I want the entire state government to do everything we can to combat this virus," I said.

This was it. For weeks, we had been working to learn all we could about the mysterious new virus—to find as many of those missing tiles of the mosaic as possible. I personally talked with researchers and medical professionals. At every level of our state government, public health officials had been contacting medical doctors and infectious disease experts to make ourselves as prepared as we could be. We downloaded every shred of available information we could from federal officials. We held calls every day with health officials around the country and the governors of other states. With 2019's disruptive weather events fresh in our minds, I asked that we hold strategy meetings with the state's National Guard leadership as well.

Yet, for all that effort, nobody knew much of anything for certain. In those early days, our very best experts around the country—and at all levels of state and federal government—were still debating how the virus was transmitted. Was it primarily transmitted through the air? Did it come from touching infected surfaces?

Only a few days prior, our senior policy staff had gathered in the conference room in the state capitol to watch the nation's top medical expert, Dr. Anthony Fauci, dismiss the notion of wearing masks during an interview with CBS's *60 Minutes*.

"There's no reason to be walking around with a mask," Dr. Fauci assured viewers. "While masks may block some droplets, they do not provide the level of protection people think they do," he went on. "Wearing a mask may also have unintended consequences: People who wear masks tend to touch their face more often to adjust them, which can spread germs from their hands."

In late February, former US surgeon general Jerome Adams tweeted that Americans should refrain from panic-buying masks: "They are NOT effective in preventing general public from catching #Coronavirus, but if healthcare providers can't get them to care for sick patients, it puts them and our communities at risk!"

I mention these not to embarrass Dr. Adams or Dr. Fauci. My point is that COVID-19 was something nobody truly understood at the time.

Most Americans knew precious little about the origins of the virus, beyond the simple fact that it first appeared in Wuhan, China. They were uncertain how it spread. And the medical community did not know how to treat infected people.

As a leader, you always want ground truth before you act, but you don't have the luxury of waiting. You have to go forward, guided by principle. As long as you commit to adjusting as necessary—when new information comes to light, as new pieces of the mosaic are discovered—you can be confident in your decisions.

This is not easy. In fact, it's incredibly hard. Leading in a time of uncertainty is one of those things that truly test both people and their principles. In March 2020, America was about to find out who was worthy of the challenge—and who was not.

After Melissa broke the news that day in March 2020, I gathered my senior team, secretary of health, and state epidemiologist to prepare for a press conference. Our Emergency Operations Center had been up and running for months at this point. We had a plan ready. It was time to inform South Dakotans. To stay transparent.

I genuinely believed the public deserved to know everything I knew—and just as soon as I knew it. I wanted my announcement to be totally informative, leaving as little as possible for people to jump to their own conclusions and spread unnecessary fear.

I certainly didn't have all the answers. All I knew was that I had to lead. I had to assure South Dakotans that we would get through this together no matter what this virus looked like. No matter how long it lasted.

When you run for office, you never think you're signing up to lead your state through a global pandemic—except you are. As governor, there is no one else but you to make the hard decisions to protect people *and* their freedom. It's one thing to know this in an intellectual sort of a way; it's another thing entirely to have the weight of that responsibility settle on you over a matter of minutes. *Could I handle it?*

When I was a kid, my mom often quoted 2 Timothy 1:7: "For God has not given us a spirit of fear, but of power and of love and of a sound mind" (NKJV). I repeated this passage to myself over and over again all through that bleak week in March 2020, and it would stick with me for the next year and a half. Mindless fear was not an option—at least not for me. I knew that I had to have a sound mind to make unprecedented, difficult decisions. And I also knew that with God's grace and strength, I could make them.

The day after we reported South Dakota's first cases, COVID-19 was officially declared a global pandemic. The next week was a long one: I spent countless hours on the phone with lawyers and legal advisers. Every single decision I made had to be within the strict confines of the authority granted me by the US Constitution and the Constitution of the State of South Dakota. And—not that I needed a lawyer to tell me this—shutting down my entire state and confining people to their homes did not fall into that category.

Obviously, I desperately wanted to help people. But abusing my powers as governor was not the right way. Striking the right balance was a never-ending challenge.

One Saturday morning in late March, my family and I had gathered in the kitchen at the governor's residence in gloomy silence. We were all exhausted.

Suddenly, Kassidy sat up. "I'm going for a run," she said. "Who wants to come?"

"I do," I said.

"Me too," said Kennedy.

The three of us changed clothes and headed out into the chilly day. We ran until sheer exhaustion got the better of us. As our run became a walk, we passed Scooter's Coffee on Sioux Avenue.

"Let's grab coffee for our walk back," I suggested. The girls immediately agreed. No one in the Noem family ever refuses coffee, and to paraphrase the expression about tea, there's really no problem that can't be made just a little better with a hot cup of coffee.

Or so I hoped.

Scooter's in Pierre has only a drive-thru, and as there were few cars already in line, we jumped in behind them. That's when we saw that people, sitting in their personal vehicles, were wearing rubber gloves: these drivers were so afraid they didn't want to risk touching a stranger's hand even by accident while passing a credit card or taking a coffee cup through an open window. I knew it then, beyond any doubt: *this virus is going to reach deep into our everyday lives.*

We all had lumps in our throats, but when we walked up to the window to order, dressed in our workout gear and shivering from the cold, we saw people in the cars in front and behind us beginning to smile. We even got a few laughs from the barista behind the window. Looking in, we saw the workers chatting cheerfully to themselves, working fast to make drinks and fill orders.

A second realization hit me then: *We will figure out a way through all this fear and uncertainty. We'll work together, just like we did in the storms of 2019.*

Strange as it was, that people could laugh at three ridiculous women standing in a drive-thru line gave me faith. The worse the situation, the better South Dakotans rally together and press onward.

I received the daily report on South Dakota's COVID-19 deaths by 7:00 a.m. The only word for how that felt is "agonizing."

I woke every morning with a cold feeling in my stomach anticipating that information. Because we're a small state, the deaths were personal. So very often, the victim was known either to me and my family or to someone on my executive team. And in the early days of the pandemic, we sat in my office and discussed every single one. *Who was that? Where had they lived? Did they have any underlying conditions?* And hardest of all: *How is the family?*

Like countless others, I lost people dear to me. I think of them every day.

One day, I woke up to a text from a dear family friend of nearly fifty years. I will call him John. John had tested positive; he was in the hospital. It wasn't good. We stayed in touch, right up until the time he went on the ventilator. John wanted to give a window into the lived experience of those suffering from the virus in isolation. He also wanted to give an example of endless trust in the Lord's love for him and his family. He did so better than he ever realized.

From day one, our objective was to stop the spread of COVID-19. When reality and the data soon taught us that just wasn't possible, we quickly switched gears to focus on slowing the spread of the virus—flattening the curve—and buying time for hospitals and doctors and nurses to gather the resources they needed to save lives.

That is exactly what we did.

The initial projections of March 10, 2020, showed our hospitalization capacity was going to be unmanageable; we wouldn't be able to take care of everybody if they all got sick at the same time. The targeted steps we took in response pushed our peak back six months—giving our health-care workers vital time to ramp up supplies, build bed capacity, and gain a better understanding of how to treat the disease.

A key part of these efforts was the executive order I issued on March 13, declaring a state of emergency in South Dakota and directing how the state would respond. Critically, the last line of the order read as follows: "This Executive Order shall be in effect immediately and shall continue for thirty (30) days until expiration on April 12, 2020, unless sooner terminated or extended in writing."

On April 28, 2020, I made another decision, one I regard as among the most important of my time as governor: I decided it was time to return to normal operations. The virus was still with us, and I would continue doing everything within my power to combat it, but *I would not seize more power.* I determined those emergency powers that I had relied upon in the very first days of the pandemic were no longer justified. Following my second principle—know government's true limits—I gave them up.

I had no idea that political forces far outside South Dakota would soon make that decision, our state, and yours truly a flashpoint in a nationwide fight over the limits of government authority in people's lives. It became national news.

I admit I was stunned by the vitriol that swiftly flowed my way from the media, Democrats, and even fellow Republicans over my refusal to go along with the draconian lockdowns and mandates other governors were issuing. But I made my decisions based on the simple faith that if the citizens of my state were armed with all the information available, they would make the best decision about their own health and the health of their families. Period.

I still don't believe my decision to keep South Dakota open should have been national news. As governor, I can make only decisions within the limits of my constitutional authority.

Amid the media frenzy that April, I distinctly remember thinking to myself: *When leaders overstep their authority, that is how we lose a country.*

What we needed was for people to remember our history and our Constitution. We needed to recognize that it's every American's responsibility to safeguard our freedom, and not just for ourselves, but for future generations. Because freedom is incredibly fragile. Once gone, it is very hard to get it back.

In those early months, it was my practice every day—sometimes twice daily—to go in front of state and national media to provide detailed updates on everything our team knew and was doing about COVID-19 in South Dakota.

I gave the public the facts, the science, and the data behind every one of my decisions. I walked through our models and projections. I took hundreds of questions.

Still, for some in the media and the political world this was not good enough. Most days, it felt as if no matter what I did or said, the political left and their media allies were on the attack simply because I was sticking to my second principle of knowing government's true limits. Pandemic or no, politics never stops.

I don't complain about it; this is part of the job. But I was incredibly frustrated. So, one day I decided to do something different. Instead of reading from charts, I spoke from the heart. As a neighbor, not a governor.

"For weeks, we've all been glued to the news searching for updates about COVID-19," I said. "We have the knowledge and the resources of modern medicine that give us the tools to defeat this, as we have so many other illnesses that we've dealt with in the past, from polio to the flu...But I want to ask you to pause and take a step back."

I shared a story from one of my staffers. At the grocery store checkout line, she had asked the woman behind the register how she was doing. Tears suddenly welled up in the cashier's eyes. "I'm really scared," she said. For several minutes, the cashier gave voice to her fears, telling a total stranger what kept her awake at night because she just needed to talk to someone.

"That cashier speaks for so many of us," I told the people gathered for the briefing. I reminded them of the emotional toll of isolation—already a hard reality in a rural state like South Dakota.

"So please...put down your smartphones, turn off your TVs...Spend time with your family. Call a loved one. Just take a break. Focus on the good things that you have in your life—the blessings...A threat like this can break us down, or it can make us truly appreciate the many blessings that we do have."

I continued, "It's okay to be uncertain, but at the same

time, we can also pour ourselves into our families, into our neighbors, and into our communities. People are afraid, and they're worried. And some may be losing hope. But my message to you is hang in there. We will get through this, and we will persevere."

Despite the fear, I believed we could grow closer together through this pandemic. "If there's anything that we all can rally around today, it's that we all have a common enemy—and that's this virus," I said.

Not long after, I decided to take my own advice: Bryon and I decided to take our family to the Badlands to hike for a day, just so we could be together. I got up early on a Sunday and packed a picnic lunch (not something I'm known to do), and we drove out together.

If you have never been to the Badlands, there is a power in its sweeping vistas of layered rock that reminds you that, for all of humankind's mesmerizing achievements, we did not make ourselves or our world, that there is a Creator who made this earth and us out of love. As I hiked that rugged terrain with my husband and our children, I realized what I wanted to remind people of at that briefing: Don't let fear crowd out your love for the people in your life. The three things that matter most are faith, hope, and love, "but the greatest of these is love" (1 Cor. 13:13).

I believe my message resonated that day in South Dakota.

Boy, do I wish I could say the same for the rest of the country.

*   *   *

The stupidity was breathtaking. From the outset, government officials—especially in Washington—were pinwheels of conflicting information, advice, and orders—orders I believe they had no power to give in the first place.

Masks were useless at best, until they became our only hope.

Everyone needed to stay indoors, until everybody needed to be outdoors.

President Trump was "racist" and "xenophobic" for trying to shut down travel from China, where the virus originated.

Vaccines, according to Democrats and some government officials, would take years to develop, until private companies developed them within months and suddenly you were an ignorant person if you didn't immediately go get one.

If you've ever read George Orwell's books, such as *1984* or *Animal Farm*, it was the same mindless seesawing of messaging from government officials that made those stories so terrifying. Except this wasn't fiction; it was real life.

With the stupidity came a blinding arrogance—especially when it came to dividing people into "essential" and "nonessential" workers. This was something even Republican governors got caught up in. To my way of thinking, any American who gets up and goes to work every day is essential, whether your job is caring for the sick, driving a delivery truck, stocking a shelf, or milking a herd of cows. You matter. And your job matters because it matters *to you*.

*   *   *

For millions of Americans, life will never return to normal: the virus stole husbands and wives, parents and grandparents, children, neighbors, friends. In one of the great, unspeakable tragedies of our time, many of them died alone, without the comfort of their loved ones in their final moments on this earth. For the living, the agony of isolation compounded their grief. Cruelly, many families were denied even the closure and solace of a funeral service.

Americans were forced to grieve alone.

What have we learned? In the face of such pain, it is a difficult but absolutely necessary question to answer. We have all learned more than we ever wanted to know about coronaviruses and masks and vaccines. We have learned that frontline medical providers—nurses, paramedics, and doctors—are among the most dedicated, heroic, and least appreciated people in our country. But the greatest lesson is one we should have known from the very start: the best way to fight a virus—or any danger to our country—is through an informed and free American people that makes decisions for themselves.

The third principle I strove to follow throughout the pandemic was to trust the people of South Dakota. Americans will always know their needs better than government. This is the very definition of self-governance. No distant administrator, however brilliant, informed, or well intentioned, can ever know the needs of a family better than that family. And no governor either, for that matter.

I have never regretted my decision to refuse unconstitutional powers over South Dakotans. My trust in them was well placed. They proved responsible, resilient, and courageous. Because we never gave up our basic rights, our way of life has been largely restored, and our economy is booming at the time I write this in late 2021.

We never closed our economy. We never issued mask mandates. We never kept anybody from going to church or singing hymns. As governor, I did not dictate to the people of South Dakota what they could or could not do. I did not arrest, ticket, or fine a single individual for exercising their basic rights as free Americans.

South Dakota ended up being the only state that never divided private businesses into "essential" or "nonessential" categories. As I told South Dakotans many times during those months, if you're essential on Tax Day, you're essential every other day of the year too.

As I mentioned at the beginning of this book, South Dakota's state motto is "Under God the People Rule." We lived up to that in spirit and deed. I believe our response to the pandemic was our finest hour. Because as we look around at the world now, we see what can only be described as an evaporation of fundamental freedoms as a direct consequence of the COVID lockdowns. South Dakota does not have that problem.

All the same, there was not a single decision in all this time that was easy.

People were dying.

Families were losing loved ones.

I think about them *every day*. I expect I will for the rest of my life. For all the guidance and help you receive as governor, there is no advice anyone can give that will prepare you for this. It is inextricably part of the job. You must accept it, and you must do your best. As I noted at the beginning of this chapter, real leadership is principled decision-making, but it is very often a lonely business.

Chapter 21

America's Fireworks

Mount Rushmore is a shrine to America's great outdoors. Like all our national parks, it reminds us that our country was built out of wilderness, and our mountains, forests, and rivers of the great interior shaped our national character and our destiny.

American history, with all its promise and complexity, is embodied in Mount Rushmore. A massive undertaking, the carving of the four heads took place between 1927 and 1941. At one point, Lewis and Clark, the explorers of the American West who founded the first American settlement in South Dakota in 1804, were going to be featured. Ultimately, the designers settled on the four presidents for very specific reasons.

George Washington honors the nation's founding. Thomas Jefferson, who negotiated the Louisiana Purchase, represents our growth as a republic. Abraham Lincoln, who saw the young country through its greatest crisis, stands for its preservation. And the visionary Teddy Roosevelt, who took office early in a new century, is a tribute to the nation's future development.

As governor of South Dakota, part of my job is to protect my state's unique history. It is an imperfect history. We should have the humility to grapple with our common past and understand that the men and women who settled the South Dakota frontier were not without their faults. Those four presidents, great as they were, were not perfect. Neither was the man who carved Mount Rushmore, sculptor Gutzon Borglum.

But we must also have the courage to acknowledge the extraordinary achievements of those who came before us, who overcame incredible adversity, and who made unimaginable sacrifices to build the country we have today.

Yes, American history is complicated and hard. *All* history is complicated and hard. Human life, past and present, is never simple. Every family history is checkered, to some extent, and with great inheritances come humbling challenges. But I believe Americans are brave enough to face those challenges, to overcome adversity, celebrate our triumphs—to be a *teachable people* who learns from our history and goes confidently into the future with, as Lincoln said, "malice toward none and charity for all."

As the summer of 2020 wore on, and as we came closer to the Fourth of July, it became clear that our country was considering a question central to our identity: *Is America worth celebrating?* To me, the answer was—and remains—undoubtedly, yes.

But powerful forces in the country disagreed, and our conflicting views would meet in a fierce fight that went right to the granite core of Mount Rushmore itself.

In December 2018, shortly after I was elected governor, President Trump invited several governors-elect to Washington to talk about our priorities and see where he might be able to help. Before the trip, I asked my senior staff and cabinet members to compile an extensive memo with several requests that I could bring to his attention.

When I arrived at the White House, we were escorted to the Cabinet Room where my fellow governors and I made small talk and shared campaign stories while we waited for the president. When President Trump came in, he shook hands with each of us, then asked us to be seated around the enormous mahogany table so the press could come in. After a few introductory remarks and a couple of questions, the press were escorted out so we could get down to business.

I had worked closely with President Trump while serving in Congress. Having seen him make decisions on a range of issues, I had a good understanding of what made him tick. Put simply, he was a doer. To take full advantage of this moment, I needed to be clear, concise, definitive, and passionate. *Top three. What are my top three most important things right at this moment?* I asked myself.

Knowing the president's bias for action, I understood that bringing up matters we could tackle right off the bat would increase the chances of getting them done. They would also be far more likely to warrant the president's personal involvement.

We went around the room, each governor talking about their priorities and the specific issues they were dealing with in their states. I began to notice, however, that few of my colleagues had come with specific requests.

Seated beside the president, I was one of the last to speak. When my clock started ticking, the president turned to me.

"Congratulations, Kristi," he said. "You had a tough race. But you pulled it out when I came in and helped you, didn't you? Good job. Good job. What can I do for you?"

I jumped into my three asks.

"Mr. President, I need a farm bill and trade agreements done. Our farmers and ranchers need access to new markets to level out the playing field to continue to grow our nation's food supply."

The president nodded.

"I'd also like to have your help with moving some opportunity zones," I went on.

More nodding.

"And lastly, Mr. President," I said, "I'd like your help getting fireworks back to Mount Rushmore."

He immediately perked up. "Fireworks? What do you mean?"

I told him that South Dakota had a long tradition of a fireworks celebration on top of Mount Rushmore every

Fourth of July eve. But for ten years, I explained, the display had been canceled—ever since the Obama administration had barred them, claiming that the fireworks might trigger "environmental concerns."

"Mr. President, this is South Dakota's one opportunity to really become the focus of the nation for one night each year." I explained how every news network and media outlet, and sometimes even international news, would play clips of the fireworks show the next day, Independence Day. Bringing fireworks back to Mount Rushmore would be an incredible tribute to freedom in our country—a western sky lit with red, white, and blue fireworks illuminating some of our nation's greatest leaders. Beyond that, tourism is South Dakota's second-largest industry. Marketing our state on national television on America's birthday had always been incredibly beneficial for us.

It made sense to President Trump. And from that moment on, he was *fixated* on getting us our fireworks back.

My team and I worked diligently with the Department of Interior and the White House for almost two years straight on logistics and planning. Every time I saw President Trump in that time, without fail, he would ask, "Kristi, how are we coming along on our fireworks?"

"We are working it, Mr. President," I assured him.

The truth was that bureaucrats within his own administration were trying to stop it. For starters, the National Park

Service (NPS) did not want to facilitate the event. Getting one of their senior leaders to agree even to a *meeting* about the event required a special trip for them out to the national monument. NPS staff brought up fire concerns, water-quality concerns, cultural concerns, and, once the pandemic hit, health concerns. At one point, a staffer even asked, "How could this event offend people on Twitter?"

I kid you not.

There's an old expression in Washington that "people are policy." That is 100 percent true. And there was one person in particular who held a significant amount of power over the planning process and was not keen on this event.

My office made repeated requests to meet with Secretary of the Interior David Bernhardt to get an agreement signed, permits obtained, and the planning process underway. When Secretary Bernhardt was slated to speak at the Western Governors Association in Vail, Colorado, in June 2019, I finally had an opportunity to speak with him directly.

Usually at these conferences, each governor gets a chance to meet with the participating officials to discuss issues important to their state. I had requested a meeting with the secretary to discuss a duck hunting provision for South Dakota, but as it amended federal rules on the sport, I needed the federal government's help. Once I was done making my pitch to the secretary, I told him that I wanted to discuss one other important topic—fireworks over Mount Rushmore.

"Yeah, I figured," the secretary replied bluntly.

I was describing the lack of support we'd gotten from our federal partners when he interrupted me.

"Do you want the duck hunting changes or the fireworks?" Bernhardt asked. "You can't have both."

He knew I was a passionate hunter and how much hunting meant to the people of South Dakota, so I'm guessing he knew how hard this was to hear.

"Why not?" I asked. "The president said we could do both."

Secretary Bernhardt was clearly skeptical, and quite frankly I got the impression he was hoping I would choose the duck hunting changes. But I stuck to my guns (so to speak). I demanded both. To his credit, Secretary Bernhardt did eventually come around. By the end, he became one of our biggest champions for celebrating American independence by returning fireworks to Mount Rushmore.

Still, it was months after my June meeting with Secretary Bernhardt before we heard anything from the federal government. Stop and think about that for a minute. The president of the United States—the "leader of the free world"—was in favor of returning fireworks to Mount Rushmore. The secretary of interior—who was appointed by the president—was in favor of returning fireworks to Mount Rushmore. And—not for nothing—the governor of the state in which Mount Rushmore exists was in favor of returning fireworks to Mount Rushmore.

And yet, it was nearly impossible to get this event through a massive, unelected federal bureaucracy that didn't want it.

*　　*　　*

It is never just a simple yes with the federal government. Everything is always draped in miles and miles of red tape. For us to have fireworks at Mount Rushmore, the federal government insisted on elaborate requirements.

It was absurd. Environmental studies needed to be conducted. Federal permits needed to be obtained. Extensive back-burning had to occur on all the surrounding Forest Service land. We needed numerous sign-offs and agreements between all the key players, including Mount Rushmore officials, South Dakota Wildland Fire, Black Hills community leaders, local law enforcement, South Dakota Department of Public Safety, South Dakota National Guard, South Dakota Department of Agriculture, South Dakota Department of Environment and Natural Resources, South Dakota Department of Tribal Relations—and our nine tribes.

And then—because President Trump had expressed interest in showing up—all those agencies had to reach agreements with the United States Secret Service. After all, there might be protests.

Then came the engineers who had to determine exactly where we would set up the fireworks display. This wasn't like the areas where we blow off rockets and Roman candles in our front yards on the Fourth of July. This was a place in which dozens of pallets would be constructed and hundreds of metal mortars would be placed to secure the pyrotechnics and keep the memorial and spectators safe all while creating a fantastic show.

And, of course, the weather.

We developed a go/no-go checklist to help both the state and the federal governments to stay accountable to their commitment of making this a safe event. This checklist included fire preparedness levels, local burn levels and probability rates, wind speed at the site of the launch, and the assurance that all parties involved were still comfortable with proceeding.

Over the course of this planning period, three different people came into the position of superintendent of Mount Rushmore. Each new person brought new concerns and a fresh face to make us worry about the viability of the event.

You would think we were launching astronauts into space with all the hoops we jumped through, when in reality it was a fireworks show like those we had done flawlessly *for years* until the Obama administration quashed it.

Jim Hagen, my cabinet secretary for South Dakota's Department of Tourism; Wanda Goodman, Jim's deputy secretary; and my daughter Kennedy—doubling as the federal government liaison in my office—worked with the Department of Interior and the National Park Service on a daily basis to fulfill requirements, answer questions, facilitate meetings, and meticulously plan every detail.

Worst of all was the organized, nationwide campaign in the spring and summer of 2020 to rip down references to our nation's founding and other points in history. From coast to coast, this was a movement that intentionally focused exclusively on our forefathers' flaws, and that purposefully ignored their virtues. I believed then and believe now that this was done deliberately to discredit America's principles to remake our country into a different political image. The attempt to "cancel" the founding generation was an attempt to cancel our freedoms.

One day, early in the summer of 2020, as the whole nation convulsed with fights over identity politics and extreme levels of political correctness, I came across a segment on cable news that remains one of the most mind-boggling displays of ignorance I've ever seen on television—and that's saying something. Standing in the Black Hills, with the iconic chiseled images of four US presidents behind her, CNN correspondent Leyla Santiago described the impending visit of the president of the United States to one of America's most popular tourist attractions this way:

> President Trump will be at Mount Rushmore, where he'll be standing in front of a monument of two slave owners and on land wrestled away from Native Americans. I'm told that...he'll be focusing on the effort to "tear down our country's history."

It's worth noting that if it were not for the four men carved into the stone behind her, Leyla would be living a very different life in a very different country. The very rights she mindlessly enjoys today—such as getting to say whatever careless thing she wants—would not exist if not for the men who set the foundation for freedom as we know it. What's more, President Obama had visited Rushmore only a few years before—without any such criticism from the media. It was just more hypocrisy and total loss of objectivity from the media.

The reporter had no idea that she was proving the point about the need to protect our treasured history from ignorant vandals. She was standing there on national television attacking our history to smear Republicans and patriotic Americans as racist, uncaring, and generally supportive of slavery and genocide. Her report was more than just an attack on the Founders, it was an assault on every American who cherishes our history.

Sitting there watching her babble on, I could not help but take it personally. This was, after all, my home state. And, as South Dakota's governor, preserving this revered national landmark was part of my responsibility.

If the Left wants to come after Mount Rushmore, they're going to have to go through me.

The president of the United States and his family were coming. Making it all the more exciting—and challenging—the White House offered to do a flyover of both Air Force One and Marine One. (President Trump certainly knew how to make an entrance!) The question became how to safely accommodate the crowd in the valley at the foot of the mountain. In the end, we decided to offer 7,500 tickets to the public—to be distributed via a lottery system.

More than 125,000 people signed up in three days.

On July 3, 2020, President Trump and his family arrived at Ellsworth Air Force Base, just east of Rapid City. Air Force One did a flyover at Mount Rushmore before landing, a special treat for the early attendees in the crowd below.

I welcomed the president and First Lady on the runway at Ellsworth. From there we would ride on Marine One to Mount Rushmore and land at the park's helipad before making our way to the Sculptor's Studio to meet the rest of our families and the congressional delegation.

"Welcome to South Dakota Mr. President," I said as he and Melania came down the steps. I was standing a politically correct six feet away, despite negative COVID tests. It was ridiculous, but at this point, I was past caring. After nearly two years, what began with a conversation between the president and me in the Cabinet Room at the White House had finally come to pass.

President Trump waved for me to join him and we turned for Marine One.

For all the times I have gazed at the faces of Mount Rushmore, I have never seen them quite like I did that day from the inside of Marine One. The skill of the Marine pilots was incredible; they got us *close*. I remember being eye-to-eye with the spectacles of our nation's twenty-sixth president—the conservationist, naturalist, historian, and "Rough Rider" Theodore Roosevelt.

Teddy would have loved this, I thought.

Adding to the drama, the production team was playing the radio communications of the helicopter pilots over the loudspeakers so the crowd could hear their commands and approach. As we flew past, the crowd below began cheering. Looking down, I saw people dancing.

People needed this, I realized. We all did. After months of a global pandemic, this was the first time for so many that they had done anything that felt normal—human.

We were Americans, together again.

My mother was in the audience that day. Later, she told me that looking around the crowd, she saw tears streaming down the faces of the people around her. No masks. No fear. Just profound gratitude for the gift of living in this country.

After meeting our families and local dignitaries in the Sculptor's Studio, it was time for the program to begin. The United States Air Force Band welcomed the president and First Lady to the stage with the playing of "Hail to the Chief," followed by the national anthem. Next came a series of flyovers with aircraft from the South Dakota National Guard and the different branches of the military. The air show was punctuated with a stunning performance by the Blue Angels and a screaming precision approach from behind Mount Rushmore.

The whole display of freedom, power, and might was spectacular.

The speeches began with Secretary Bernhardt. Then it was my turn. I shamelessly promoted South Dakota and its fundamentally good people. Then I borrowed words from Teddy Roosevelt—a leader who appreciated good people, flaws and all: "It is not the critic who counts—not the man who points out how the strong man stumbles. Or where the doer of deeds could have done better. The credit belongs to the man who is actually in the arena, whose face is marred by dust and sweat and blood, who strives valiantly, who errs and comes up short again and again because there is no effort without error or shortcoming. But who knows great enthusiasms, the great devotions, who spends himself for a worthy cause."

Boy, you'd be hard-pressed to find a better quote for our times.

"On this Independence Day, let us be grateful that we have such words and such examples to follow," I went on, "that others were willing to sacrifice so much to create a land in which liberty and law can be protected. Let us not destroy our history. Let us learn from it by preserving and celebrating what was great and fixing what was not."

I then issued a call to action for those gathered in the canyon—and for anyone else watching that night. "We must all renew our commitment to a country where any person, regardless of his or her standing at birth, can make anything of themselves. Like me. I was just a farm kid. Now I am the first female governor of South Dakota. Let us all, like our founding fathers, pledge our own lives, our fortunes, our sacred honor, to the cause of liberty and self-government. So that we may continue to have the freedom to follow our conscience, to build our lives, and to live in peace."

The fireworks that night were something out of this world. The sound echoed off the Black Hills like endless rolls of thunder. In the flashes of their dazzling light, I could see thousands of people, from all across America, watching in wonder.

This was a defiant celebration of life—the life of a nation, born from desperate beginnings—and a celebration of the lives of everyone continuing that story now despite a global pandemic—those gathered in the canyon below and those all across the country.

Further, in the months leading up to the Fourth of July, the country had seen so many angry people tearing down monuments from our past, believing they could only be sources of pain and division. Here at Mount Rushmore, we had the opposite. The isolation and fear of the pandemic had been heavy on us all. Here, for the first time in so long, people had come together.

We want to be united as much as we want to be free, I remember thinking to myself.

In that moment, I knew in my heart: our country will survive.

Whatever comes, whatever trials from within or without, we can rest assured that the human heart never stops yearning for true freedom, and it never stops yearning for true community. That freedom is not a license to act on whatever whim, but the ability to serve, honor, and love the good things, the true things, the beautiful things. And that community is not something that can be forced on us by official authority, but something that must be freely chosen. Something given.

Human nature then was on our side, just as our Founders believed it was on theirs when they set up this country so long ago. That alone won't be enough to see us through, to fix those things still broken about us. That will be our job. But we're up for it.

We're Americans, after all, and we don't complain about things. We fix them.

Epilogue

In June 2021, Bryon and I became grandparents. Our daughter Kassidy and her husband, Kyle, welcomed into the world their beautiful baby girl, Adeline West, named after my grandmother. Weighing 7 pounds, 14 ounces and all of 20 inches long, she was total perfection, with *lots* of hair.

Just like that, our lives changed again. And I got a new title: "Mema."

Of the many roles and responsibilities Bryon and I have shared these last thirty years, being grandparents is by far the best. There is nothing quite like seeing your children become parents. And it's true what they say: as a grandmother, you get all the fun of delighting in a beautiful baby—but come nighttime, you can hand this precious little bundle back. (Although I admit, that's usually pretty hard for me to do. I *definitely* hog the baby.)

I am so unbelievably grateful for this little baby and our family. I am equally determined that our country and the world will be a better place for Adeline to grow up. Every parent feels this, and I'm keenly aware that I've been blessed with an opportunity to play a role in that work. I think about this responsibility every day.

My own father did not live to see his grandchildren. Sometimes, I wonder what he would have told them...or me. If I could take one last ride with him now—maybe to that patch of native ground he bought so long ago, where the lavender pasqueflowers bloom beside the snowbanks—I wonder what Dad would say about our family and the farm.

About South Dakota and its people.

About our country and its future.

I don't know for sure, but I can imagine him saying something like this: "There's a lot that needs fixing still, Kristi, and we're burning daylight. But it will be a better day tomorrow."

Acknowledgments

I owe a debt of gratitude to the people of South Dakota for entrusting me to serve them in public life for nearly twenty years now. This book is really about them—their unique and absolutely essential way of life, the challenges they face, and the limitless faith they show in meeting those obstacles. They prove the truth of our state motto: "Under God the people rule."

Charlie Hurt was the first person who convinced me my life was interesting enough that people would want to read about it. After reading a few chapters, Charlie would call me up laughing—and proceed to ask a dozen different questions. I don't consider myself a writer, but answering those questions gave me the first half of this book before I knew it. He is a great friend.

Beth Hollatz took a chance on a young mom, quit her job, and jumped in my pickup to campaign for Congress with me because she believed we could win when no one else did. I've never met anyone more passionate, loyal, or inspiring than Beth. She is a great American, and I love her dearly.

Acknowledgments

I have to thank my lieutenant governor, Larry Rhoden. I expect it's difficult at times for a West River rancher to play second fiddle to a young woman from farm country in the eastern part of the state. But Larry always respected my decisions, argued with me when someone needed to, gave wise counsel, and at the end of the day no matter what, has been my friend. Thank you, Larry.

My sister Cindy picked up everything I dropped when I ran for Congress in 2010. She took over my children's pastor duties at church and helped run the 4-H club I had led. She baked my kids' treats for school and took care of my ranch and house. She is my best friend. I may run the state of South Dakota, but Cindy runs my life. She is amazing. When I grow up, I want to be just like her.

I could not have asked for better brothers than Robb and Rock. As just one small example: Robb calls me every day just to "check on me."

God has put several "encouragers" in my life to lift me up and keep me in the fight each day. I want to thank them for the texts and emails on tough days, the phone calls that made me laugh when I didn't think I could, and prayers they sent up on our family's behalf. Kelly and my prayer warriors, Pastor Jeanne and the "happy church," Al and Sharon Noem, our church family, Steve Kirby, Harvey Jewett, Shawn DeWitt, Kim Winter, Greg Anderson, Virginia's Silver Bullets, Ed Randazzo, John Wiik, Roger and Barb Fritz, and Foster and Lynn Friess. They have never quit on me.

Acknowledgments

I have the best staff with me in the governor's office and an amazing political team. They are fighters who are in the fight for all the right reasons. I'm so thankful for them each day.

This book is a collection of my personal reflections, but it would not have been possible without the dedicated help of a highly talented team. Across the lifecycle of this book Matt Latimer and Dylan Colligan at Javelin Literary Agency gave sage guidance. They especially encouraged me to remain focused on the enduring human stories and personal lessons of this book, and not the day-to-day political battles that can seem so important at the time. A special thanks to Bill Rivers for helping me artfully assemble some of the more meaningful stories, reminiscences, and memories contained here.

To my publisher Sean Desmond and the Hachette Book Group team, I owe a debt of gratitude for making my first introduction to the publishing industry a wonderfully warm and smooth process. In their expert hands, this South Dakota farm kid felt comfortable sharing her personal memoir with the wider literary world.

I have strived to be as accurate as possible in my recollection of the events and stories told here, and a devoted host of others have engaged to ensure the greatest degree of factual accuracy. Given that, any errors remaining are mine alone.

Lastly—and most of all—I would like to thank my

husband, Bryon, my rock, and our children, Kassidy, Kennedy, and Booker. Ours has been a family adventure unlike anything we could have expected or planned. It would not be possible without your love, support, and patience. Thank you so much, and I love you more than you know.

About the Author

KRISTI NOEM is the current governor of South Dakota. A member of the Republican Party, she was the US representative for South Dakota's at-large congressional district from 2011 to 2019 and a member of the South Dakota House of Representatives from 2007 to 2011. Noem was elected governor in 2018 and is South Dakota's first female governor.